ISBN-13:   9780988585522
BISAC CODES: OCC019000
                SEL016000
                SEL032000

This publication is designed to provide accurate and authoritative information in regard to the subject matter covered. It is sold with the understanding that the publisher is not engaged in rendering legal, accounting, or other professional service. If legal advice or other expert assistance is required, the services of a competent professional person should be sought. – From a Declaration of Principles Jointly Adopted by a Committee of the American Bar Association and a Committee of Publishers and Associations.

Some names and identifying details have been changed to protect the privacy of individuals.

All brand names and product names used in this book are trademarks, registered trademarks or trade names of their respective holders.

TVGuestpert Publishing is not associated with any product or vendor in this book.

TVGuestpert Publishing and the TVG logo are trademarks of Jacquie Jordan Inc.

TVGuestpert & TVGuestpert Publishing are subsidiaries of Jacquie Jordan Inc.

TVGuestpert & TVGuestpert Publishing are visionary media companies that seek to educate, enlighten, and entertain the masses with the highest level of integrity. Our full service production company, publishing house, management, and media development firm promise to engage you creatively and honor you and ourselves, as well as the community, in order to bring about fulfillment and abundance both personally and professionally.

Nationwide Distribution through Ingram & New Leaf Distributing Company
Book Cover by Jonathan Fong
Book Design by Lynette Ubel – Ubel Design
Photography by Blake Gardner
Edited by Stephanie Cobian, Suzette Cobian, Jackie Petruzzelli

Published by TVGuestpert Publishing
11664 National Blvd, #345
Los Angeles, CA. 90064
310-584-1504
www.TVGPublishing.com
www.TVGuestpert.com

First Printing April 2016

SPONTANEOUS
TRANSFORMATION

7 STEPS TO COPING
AND THRIVING
IN EXTREME TIMES

JENNIFER MCLEAN

DEDICATION

This book is dedicated to you…
as you hold this book in your hands
know that you have chosen a new path,
a journey to healing the old wounds
and quickening your movement
into vitality, freedom and new
possibilities. Congratulations.

It is also dedicated to my beautiful
sister Abbie, whose love and support
got me here and beyond. I miss
you every single day and I know your
hands and energy are in this book.
I know you are the whisper in the
ear of readers to get this book, and
move them into the healing you
didn't get a chance to experience
yourself while here.

ACKNOWLEDGMENTS

My life would not be where it is if it weren't for the many trainers, teachers, coaches and guides in my life. Special mentions go to Margaret Mikkelborg, who showed me that connection in safety was possible and started my road to healing. To my best friend Mary Hall, who has consistently had my back through my highs and lows, flaws and gifts; it would not have been any fun without you. Thanks to Matt Riemann who has showed me the power of my beliefs and ensured that new ones are being planted from a renewed space of equanimity and love.

My amazing team at McLean MasterWorks: Mike, Jessica, MaryCay, Matt, Julie, Rita, Jordan, and Christine. I LOVE US, and I'm so grateful that we get to play at changing the paradigm of healing, and the possibilities found through the heart. Thank you for your support, engagement and commitment to our mission of creating peace in the hearts and minds of our tribe. Thanks, also, to Alicia for your help in bringing this book to reality.

To Marilyn Mercado, the most amazing Lymphatic therapist, who has almost single handedly kept me standing.

Thanks to the team at TVGuespert Publishing, your attention to detail, amazing suggestions for improvements to the book, and undaunted enthusiasm about this project has been contagious and inspiring.

A BIG thanks goes to our AMAZING www.SpontaneousTransformation.com and SuccessSignature.com communities. Without you I would not be able to get this message into so many hands. Thank you for the ongoing co-creation and the profound support.

Finally, my life would not have been the adventure of healing it is without the amazing master teachers in the form of those antagonists in the play of my life. Thanks to these teachers that molded, framed and pushed me through challenge to seek, heal and grow.

In gratitude, Jennifer

INTRODUCTION

THE THINGS WE CARRY

Healing conversations start with understanding the mastery that is you. There is a master within you that has all the answers you have been seeking. I would be so bold as to say you are the master you are seeking.

I discovered this truth over twenty-five years ago through a system of vibrational healing that I developed called Spontaneous Transformation. The Spontaneous Transformation delivers the "healing conversations" on which the title of this book is based.

The journey that led me to develop the Spontaneous Transformation began with a migraine. It was a beast of a migraine that insisted on coming back over and over again. After years of pain, multiple doctor visits and no relief, I finally found CranioSacral Therapy – an alternative approach used by chiropractors, occupational therapists, and massage therapists to address and treat issues of chronic pain. This therapeutic process led me on a journey of inquiry that inspired me to study the healing modalities of Polarity Therapy, which is rooted in ancient Eastern philosophies. Its focus is on balancing the natural flow of energy in the body. I also studied Reiki Therapy, a source of restoration which, again, seeks to renew a healthy energy flow through a technique called Palm Healing. Through these studies and transformative experiences, a theme emerged – *the body is a miraculous vessel of holding.*

The body holds all of our thoughts and experiences. It also holds all the energy and wisdom we need to restore its healthy functioning. There are several ways which the body "holds" for us and those ways can either help or hinder. For example, we have all experienced sleepless nights when we tossed and turned in bed, fretting over the next day's to-do list. Those "must-do's" marched across our brain like anxious soldiers on a mission: "You must drop the kids off, then stop by the cleaners, then go to work, then get this project in by ten…" Perhaps this army of thoughts became quite aggressive and anxious: "How will I…when will I…how can I get this all done?" Our hearts raced along to these internal statements, perhaps our chests constricted, as we tossed and turned for hours. We even toss and turn through our days. These stressful thoughts, worry, overwhelm and anxiety that we are holding are the very things preventing us from moving forward in many areas of our lives.

Perhaps we have been out on a romantic dinner with our significant other or lover. While the restaurant was picked with care and the food excellent, we were too busy dwelling on yesterday's verbal slight that cut so deep and hurt so bad, that we couldn't enjoy the present moment. In fact, we could no longer really hear what our significant other was saying because we're fuming inside while holding onto so much resentment! These are examples of our body holding onto emotions from everyday experiences. If it is true that we hold these small experiences in our body, could it be that we also hold key traumas and events we've experienced in our body as well? My therapeutic experience has shown that to be the case exactly. Traumas and events from the past fuel the recent resentments and current confusion; all of it ultimately limiting our capacity to enjoy our lives to their fullest in the present.

The bigger issues we face throughout our lives pile on top of our existing daily challenges. We have all faced survival issues at some point in our lives, if not on an ongoing basis. These include financial and health challenges, pain, fear, abandonment, abuse, neglect… and now, on top of all of this, global crises. We find ourselves in the midst of hard economic times, increasing unemployment, global instability and rapid change. We live in extreme times. We face the unknown. And we absolutely need a way to stay centered and let go of all the angst and worry that threatens to throw us off course or pull us down.

Author and Vietnam vet, Tim O'Brien, wrote a short story called, "The Things We Carry," based on his experience as a soldier in the Vietnam War. This story describes the literal and emotional "things" the soldiers carried with them as they humped through the jungle. Each soldier had something that they held onto as a buffer for dealing with reality. For one soldier, it was letters from a girl he had a crush on. These letters helped to transport him into a world of daydreams in which he was romantically involved. He held on to these daydreams as a way to avoid having his head in the war. Of course, who wouldn't want to dream about a romantic relationship at home as a way to buffer the horrific reality of the present? This isn't a judgment. The analogy here is that: what he held onto in his mind affected his experience of reality.

We, too, travel through our lives carrying things, which color our experience. We all carry our experiences of love, and the failures of those who were supposed to love us. Perhaps we carry abuse, hurt, abandonment, and anger. Whatever perceptions and judgments, memories and imagined experiences – positive or negative, we carry around with us, they all shape our vision of the world and the nature of our life's journey. What we carry with us from day to day in our hearts and in our minds can make everyday life harder or easier for us, depending on how we hold onto it. If we hold onto something that evokes emotional discomfort, it can then be held in the body over time as physical discomfort.

Interestingly, the body sees itself as doing you a huge service by holding onto these things. It holds onto events and the resulting beliefs andthoughts in a subconscious capacity as a form of protection. It protects you from the confusion, upset and trauma that created energetic crossed wires and confused beliefs so that you can continue on, live and survive. The body holds FOR YOU in actual partnership with you.

This holding and protecting shows up outside of you as the events and challenges and lower-vibrating emotions that present themselves in your everyday life. These life events and reactions of anger, jealousy, upset etc., represent the areas of holding within that are ready to be noticed, explored and nudged into consciousness. Upsets (emotional, physical and mental) show up to get your attention and bring you to the areas within that are READY to be explored. We know that you are absolutely, beyond a shadow of a doubt, ready BECAUSE these events and emotions have showed up. Your body now becomes this beautiful partner beckoning you within to explore these holdings and re-aligning you into a new, clearer truth of who you are. A truth that the past events clouded with confusion for your protection (and appropriately, I might add).

The opportunity as you will discover in this book is to move your attention back to these areas of holding to re-align the energy and, in the process, release the held energy – moving from surviving to thriving.

When the holding consistently and pressingly presents itself in multiple life challenges and emotional outbreaks, it's not that you are holding onto it, but that it has a hold over you. Whatever it is that you are still carrying, it is worth discovering so that you can learn from it, release it and move forward in your freedom.

How do we just let go of all the beautiful and loving, protecting debris we are carrying, so that we can experience more happiness, joy and love? After two decades of working as an energy practitioner, utilizing various therapeutic modalities and eventually creating my own – Spontaneous Transformation – I have found that the most powerful and longest-lasting release of my perceived physical, emotional and mental upset, in both my life and my clients', comes from the Spontaneous Transformation you are about to learn. It is the practice of feeling into the body's holding and exploring past traumas and emotional events to achieve understanding and subsequent clearing of whatever has accumulated and created dissonance within the body. This is the essence of Spontaneous Transformation. Engaging with these unconscious aspects of our being, and developing those loving lines of communication, allows us to then shift and transform the nature of any trauma we have carried with us. We can now live as our authentic selves. One of the greatest gifts that comes when we live authentically is that we attract the life we've always wanted. We realize our potential, which means we make it real in the world.

The wisdom of this Spontaneous Transformation is gathered from thousands of people who successfully liberated themselves from various illnesses and heartaches. I facilitate Spontaneous Transformation group sessions online as part of my monthly membership site, *MasterWorks Healing*. The Spontaneous Transformation sessions found in this book are taken from the transcripts of those sessions so that you can witness the process via real participants. You will experience them bravely, face what they are exploring within their being, using the breadcrumbs of their lives (pain, upsets, challenges, dis-ease) as the point of access to an internal dialogue. You, in turn, can experience your own process through these examples.

Each dialogue addresses a different challenge which we have all likely experienced on some level. I'd like to explain my approach a bit here to put these sessions into context since you will only be reading the individual session and not the hour-long group call in its entirety.

These shows/calls always begin with a centering meditation, which we do together, to move within and into the present moment where all change is possible. So, by the time I begin talking with the individual who volunteers to be led through the steps of a Spontaneous Transformation, they are already in a place of centeredness, a place of connection within and to the divine – a place I reference as "the sacred chamber."

Part of my own process is to use these moments to access the vibration of those who come forward to participate and represent the soul catalyst of the group (including you, in this moment – you are part of this soul group). My responses are felt within me, which I have learned to trust. And my way of knowing and discerning has been verified and strengthened throughout several decades of participants' and clients' experiences. So, if something I say within the conversation seems like a leap in logic, it may be because I am reading into a vibrational resonance that is present within the group that is experiencing the frequency (which is present for you, too).

I also like to use "play" and "pretend" to lead our minds in a direction we might not have otherwise gone, moving toward the imagining of our needs fulfilled. The scenarios I present open us up to entertain greater possibilities for ourselves. Since the body doesn't register any difference between an imagined experience and a real one, I like to take advantage of our own under-utilized power of perspective to get us further down the path of seeing and experiencing the same issue or situation in a new way. As you will see, pretending takes each of us directly to where our soul wanted to go in the first place. It gets our bodies familiar with this new place, creating a new energetic signature of the highest qualities of health, wholeness, abundance, etc., so that we can access these qualities again at any time.

You will also notice that, at times, I ask the participants to physically tap on their heart area. This is part of a technique I use when we are preoccupied with "heady" thoughts to get each of us more grounded in our body's sensation and wisdom and bring us into the moment. Participants experience the full technique that involves tapping into the body prior to their Spontaneous Transformation session, so that they, and each of us, are aware that it is meant to center us back into our heart and into our physical experience in the present moment. You can do the same – use a centering technique before moving into your body and the Spontaneous Transformation process.

Also, one last thing... *The body experiences through its senses.* So, I often use sight, touch, and sound (and sometimes even smell) to help participants gain entry into their bodies. For example, I may ask them, "What do you see there?" Or, "What is the sensation or feeling?" Or "What is it telling you?" But everyone has a predominant way they tend to receive information – visually, kinesthetically or auditorily. Whichever it is for you, I recommend that, as you read through each session, you use the wording/ approach that works best for you.

As you travel through these participants' processes with them, you will discover just how much we all share in common. Though you may not relate to every single story, you can delve into your own related issues as I facilitate them into their body's knowing. Each participant bravely faced their own personal issues and found the next, deeper level of relief and resolution by learning what they needed within themselves in order to progress forward in their evolution. In gaining that clarity, they moved their energy, their voice, their health and their lives forward. I prefer to use "forward" instead of getting "back."

You will experience how the step-by-step process of Spontaneous Transformation works so that you can begin to lead yourself on this same path whenever you feel the need to better understand your experience. Or when an intense life moment nudges you to go inside and explore the triggered moment in a deeper way, using these upsets as a point of access to shift the energy. You may begin to recognize that, miraculously, these events and feelings that you don't want and that you perceive to be wrong or bad actually contain a gift made just for you. Each one provides another oppor- tunity for opening to your good. Each practice you learn gives you a way to embrace your challenges long enough to gain strength and understanding from them. You will experience how honoring the information found in the body, even if it is painful, and allowing the guidance that appears, actually shows us the soul's yearning of its opposite. These beautiful places of holding that may feel like pain and emotional upset are the sparkling diamonds leading us to discover their opposites – the source/divine qualities of who we really are — and which the soul is striving to express. It gets our attention through lower-vibrating emotions and life challenges. And our job is to use those moments to go within and dialogue with these aspects that are calling for our attention.

Know that just by reading this, you have begun your journey into truth. In fact, if you are holding this book, you are a catalyst person. You are part of the hundredth monkey group of individuals here to offer your increased vibration to the planet. By changing yourself, you can bring more ease and grace to the changes we are all undergoing. Our path to greater peace is through our emotions, which come from the holdings within our bodies. Deeper than any emotion, your body carries the wisdom you are now seeking. Ultimately, you have within you everything you need to move beyond any current level of surviving into actual thriving, even in extreme times. Get ready for an exciting journey as you begin feeling into deep freedom, peace, grace and love.

"Energy doesn't live, it doesn't die, it transforms."
~ Albert Einstein

TABLE OF CONTENTS

OUR BODY: ENERGY CYCLES and PATTERNS

The journey back to ourselves begins with wanting something to change.

The wonderful, fulfilling, powerful, yet dang frustrating thing about life is that it constantly shows up, nudging and pushing us inexorably to a greater state of being. What gets our attention the most? Unfortunately, it is often pain, disease, upset, anger, frustration, etc. I sincerely believe there is a time coming in the not too distant future where we will not have pain to move us. There is a time where we will be in such flow that we "see it coming" and adjust long before pain is a reality. For now, in our current evolutionary state, the appearance and perception of pain, struggle, stuckness is what will move us.

Within this model is a set of life patterns that result from our life falling into situations where we seem to have found ourselves many times before. And we wonder, *why do I even try when I always "get stuck" in the same situations?* Then, inevitably, *where do I go from here?*

The answer is: You are not stuck, nor can you ever be stuck. Stuck is simply a perception, a state of mind; it isn't real. In fact, claiming you are stuck actually stops the forward momentum of change that is attempting to get your attention. What is actually happening is life showing up for you, forever guiding you to that which you are yearning. Not stuck. Just life. AND the next step is to always go inside to seek direction and get the answers that move you forward in a positive direction.

We deepen and expand our experience each time we seek the greater learning. The opportunity found within our bodies is to broaden our angle of perception to generate a different experience. It is your chance to move from an experience of fruitless effort, stuckness, or being "up against a wall," to one of learning and curiosity, of growth, understanding and excitement for life today. This allows the exact same experience to become something that is now there *for* you, not against you. The reason I know that your current challenge is here *for* you is because you are experiencing it. Challenge is actually life itself; here to support you and nudge you in a new direction. Having this awareness brings more peace to the moment, which becomes thriving, which results in less and less of a need to experience those same struggles over and over again. In fact, the "struggle" simply becomes a place of noticing, discovery and allowing that opens you to what is next for you.

How Our Past Events and Resulting Perceptions Become Our Patterns

When we find ourselves continually dealing with the same types of perceived mistakes – relationship dynamics, addictions, diet and fitness attempts, job dissatisfaction, etc., we have the opportunity to take it on as a cycle of change. Yes, it may be a pattern that we dislike and do not enjoy, but that is exactly why we become willing to change the perception. Because, the moment we do, the pattern becomes an opportunity. The "issue" becomes the beginning of our next spectacular growth phase. Our chosen life patterns that we agreed to before we came to this incarnation are a lifelong cycle of opportunity to play, experiment, and explore in areas we want to be. Let me explain…

Our patterns will, through our life experiences, present us with the chance to conduct our own internal dialogue to discover then choose what *else* we would now prefer to experience and then move in that direction. For some, the pattern may be dating men who are controlling. Maybe the men appear different each time, yet in the end, it always comes down to the commonality among these relationships: a battle for control. Or maybe your pattern is different. Maybe you had a parent who always made you feel "not good enough," so you constantly strove to prove yourself to your parent. Now, you find yourself repeatedly in careers, friendships or relationships where you are striving to prove that you are good enough. Or perhaps you felt neglected for one reason or another, and now you lack the confidence to really make of your life what you want. So, why do these patterns occur?

Over the course of experimenting with various healing practices, I have discovered that the cyclical patterns we repeatedly experience through-out our lives are the result of past, unresolved events for which we didn't have the wherewithal or strength to manage or make sense of at the time of occurrence. The body previously experienced an event or circumstance that it is now holding until the body – you – are ready to transform it. It is not stuck in the body. It is simply stored in the body for the time and date when you have the strength and abilities to manage and explore it and, ultimately, understand it and subsequently release it. In Wiccan tradition, when you "name" something, you then own it. This is a similar principle; when you understand your pattern, there is usually compassion and allowing that leads to surrender and release.

We can only get to understanding by first becoming aware of a pattern's existence. Many of us either ignored it in the past or we perceived it as yet another life challenge, issue or problem and felt victimized by it. Yet, the reason a health issue remains, relationship patterns persist, or a certain situation repeats itself is because that part of you is calling to be recognized and released. When we don't acknowledge it, the trauma remains as something to be resolved and transmuted. It continues to hinder our energy as well as our ability to experience the health and wholeness, abundance, great relationships, fulfilling work, friendships, joy, etc., we really want and are capable of having.

The body will persistently hold these unresolved traumas as patterned thoughts and emotions that collect in the very fibers of our being until we are ready to acknowledge them and use them for our growth and expansion.

Until we go within, notice, pay attention and explore, these events or traumas tend to repeat themselves as patterns. They become like distress signals trying to alert us to their presence over and over again. Those patterns will create themselves in as many ways as it takes for you to turn your attention to them.

Patterns are not bad, nor punishment, nor karma. When we come to this planet, we come to experience life through our patterns. These patterns become the energetic fabric of this lifetime. How the pattern shows up in cycles, and how we relate to it, lets us recognize the progress of our growth or lack thereof. We may experience a specific pattern on lessening levels, or in various contexts, or we may see it play itself out in other people's lives and no longer our own. We may notice that we are less disturbed by it. These are some of the ways we know we are clearing ourselves of it because it moves further and further outside of our experience. We can make life that much easier for ourselves when we choose to look at our patterns as partners in our learning. We can work with them and grow, using each pattern as a watermark that shows us where we are within ourselves. We can try to ignore it to no end. "Getting rid of it" as fast as we can is truly not the point. The point is to embrace what is given in this lifetime and let it guide us to greater depths and heights of experience. I hear some of you at this point saying, "Dang it, I am soooo done with this freakin' pattern."

I am here to joyfully tell you that if it is still here, and you are frustrated with it, then you aren't done with it. I really do mean joyfully. For when you move your attention to one of appreciation and possibility with your patterns, they shift instantly to be a guide to your opening and you truly move into joy. It is truly that simple, but not necessarily easy. By the time you are done reading this book, you will have discovered a new found sense of "easy".

Life is Energy on the Move

I recommend that as you begin this endeavor, rather than look at issues and patterns as an unwanted experience to get rid of, approach this process with gratitude. You are about to begin a kind of conversation with your past and with what is present in your body right now. Incidents and feelings may arise that you do not even recall one hundred percent. You may only have impressions or vague sensations that an issue in your life today is related somehow to a time in your past. "What happened" isn't as important to this process as "how you hold it" now because "how you hold it" is what perpetuates it. Life is energy on the move. If you are holding onto a type of energy today, you are not allowing that aspect of yourself to move forward in the same flow as everything else that is moving.

So, it is the interpretation of the past that you're holding onto that is more important here than the past itself.

Any held events or trauma you find may have resulted from physical, emotional, mental, or spiritual injury. Through my experience working within myself and with clients, I have found that a particular energetic pattern will be stronger when it is a result of all four levels of trauma. For example, a trauma can be as dramatic as physical abuse, in which case, it is also psychological. It can also be as simple as being ignored by a parent or made to feel stupid in school. Whatever the injury, it created a holding pattern in your brain and body. Whether the significant emotional experience was repeated over time or had a powerful impact on you only once, it is now internalized in the body. These holding patterns now act as a template of associations which the mind re-accesses in any similar situation. Over time, the mind tries to make sense of what the body experienced. The thought process itself – whatever conclusions, beliefs, pain, confusion, insecurity, self-doubt, etc., we chose to derive from the trauma – can increase the negative effects, depending on how you interpreted that single event or extended circumstance. Yet, the personal assessment that you made of it in the past slipped out of conscious range into your unconscious body-mind. Though you may have forgotten it, it formed the cyclical patterns that you may be experiencing now.

Picture in your body a transparent figure, like the invisible man, outlined by a clear haze, with a river of bluish energy rushing through it. When you are healthy, this internal river of energy is flowing and gurgling and skipping along at a healthy pace. When you experience a trauma, and don't work through it, that flow gets rerouted to create side pools and "empty" spots in your energy flow. If it remains unresolved, more hurt and trauma gets absorbed and layered as stages of childhood, adolescence, and adulthood unfold. Then, through vibrational resonance (like energies are attracted to like beliefs), these patterns start creating like-experiences to get your attention. The pattern is attempting to address and have you notice and shift the emotional, physical and psychological fallout from the original event.

When you ignore the signs of your life through the challenges and pain that show up, you allow yourself to keep holding onto the old events as boulders in your stream of energy. These holdings act like filters through which you cannot help but view the world, and yourself, through those patterns and trauma-driven perspectives. Essentially, by not using these beautiful gifts of challenge to guide you to internal transformation of these holdings, you have let your past impact your perceptions to the point where it determines your future.

What I want to tell you here and now is this: You are not a victim.

You created these remarkable life adventures and patterns so that you could move through this incredible, varied experience we know as life and expand every aspect of you. There is nothing wrong with you. You are not broken or permanently damaged. These were simply things and events that happened along the way to guide you to your greater expansion. And you are ready to know this and grow; or you wouldn't be reading this now.

So, imagine this same transparent figure now as an invisible woman with a bluish haze running through her body. As this figure journeys through adolescence, perhaps her best friend steals her boyfriend. Her mind creates imagery and story around what happens. This results in a crushing feeling of betrayal, so the bluish figure absorbs the hurt into her body and it feels like a big jagged rock in her stomach. She doesn't, or can't in the moment, resolve the situation or take the time to understand her hurt feelings, so she chooses to ignore them, figuring it was a one-time deal. Then, in early adulthood, her mother dies. She feels abandoned again and absorbs this as another sharp little stone into her heart. Now her accumulated pain sticks out of her energetically at dangerous angles, becoming unapproachable and afraid she will be abandoned again. Her heart grows heavy. She develops behaviors that keep her too busy to develop close relationships, though she can't see this is what she's doing. Her energy puts people off. This is how she tries to protect herself from further loss. This is how unresolved trauma can result in all forms of unwanted experiences. The journey to a healthy energy flow involves transforming the old events that created old misunderstandings and misinterpretations into new understandings of love's presence.

Some people are traumatized by the word trauma, so it's important to clarify that "trauma" is not something bad, wrong, horrifying or awful. It is just something that happened; an event that created an overlay of belief and lower-vibrating emotions like a literal wet blanket on your energy field. Also, one person's trauma is not another's. For example, one type is not more traumatic than another. No matter what the trauma is and how it showed up and what it looked like from the outside, a trauma is a trauma for a person. Meaning a traumatic event is experienced on a deep seated and intense level for each individual, regardless of what it is. It does not need to be qualified or quantified.

Trauma, the event, the upset is whatever cries out for resolution.

For example, a client of mine, who I will call Stephanie, grew up with a father who was emotionally unavailable. Throughout adolescence and into adulthood, she found herself repeatedly involved in emotionally distant relationships. In essence, she was attracting this type of relationship by recreating this dynamic that felt safe. She absorbed that this was a safe way to love.

Another one of my clients, Marcie, had a brother who constantly teased her. The teasing felt overwhelming to her nervous system. One day she was fed up and kicked him so hard, she actually hurt her own ankle. This event spawned in her a belief that self-protection brought on pain. As she grew up, she recreated this push-pull pattern over and over again that resulted in the same kind of self-inflicted pain. Like a theme song to her life, the belief played itself out like this in every relationship she had.

How Embedded Patterns Become Life Themes

Patterns become embedded in our life's experience because the body holds our trauma to protect us from ourselves. This is really important: *the body is protecting* us so that we can continue to thrive. The mind, in turn, tucks it away. Our bodies and minds truly have our best interest at heart. They go about covering the jagged rocks of pain with the gauze of holding, which can then result in protective behaviors. It does this in order to protect us from further trauma. So the body becomes a kind of repository for all beliefs and experiences. It is a self-sustaining mechanism for our continued ability to live regardless of "what happened." Yet, if we don't address our various traumas in any real way other than to lament over them, they grow like larger boulders in a river that change the flow of our lives. We start to go out of our way to avoid what we fear will occur again. Our energy is depleted. A holding pattern develops in our body. Layers of experience begin building on this same theme from the first time it happened, perhaps at two, then again in various ways at seven and twelve and fifteen and twenty and thirty. Life repeats itself. Embedded through repetition, layers and layers form around the original trauma.

What makes our patterns seem so difficult to change is that our interpretation, which was so integral to the first occurrence of trauma, is difficult to detect – it has become our view of reality.

We universalize our perception to believe it is everyone's experience. It becomes difficult to change because we are under the impression that it's the truth and "that's just the way things are."

The good news is that it's hard to ignore a jagged rock. Meaning that, each time the pattern of pain shows up physically or emotionally, it gives us the opportunity to address the false belief made in the past because now it is present! Anything present in the body can be explored now. What was once invisible is suddenly visible in experience. The pattern is recreated to finally bring awareness to those hurting places inside, then discover the gift in them. Why am I explaining this so thoroughly? So the mind can grasp this while simultaneously allowing the heart to open to a new process of access. The Spontaneous Transformation provides this access point as a way to receive that gift. Soon you will finally be able to clearly see and release the things you carry and the things you want to leave behind.

Realign Your Energy to Transform the Pattern

When the thoughts and emotions behind the physical energy pattern are revealed, acknowledged, and released in gratitude, the body's natural intelligence takes over to re-pattern the body into balance. You return to your natural state of health and energy flow. When you are in the flow and your heart is open, the floodgates of opportunity also open. Your life is transformed because affirming new beliefs gives you a truer, unlimited perception. This not only changes the beliefs; it shifts the energy vibration which creates a sonic echo in the universe and brings to you the experiences that match that same higher-vibrating resonant energy. These new experiences affirm your truer, more complete vision of life as it is, encompassing magnificent health and wealth and happiness. This is why people who use the Spontaneous Transformation to clear and cleanse one issue often have the experience of life opening up for them in other areas at the same time – because the process goes straight to the source and core of what your soul is yearning for.

Years ago, a client of mine fully allowed herself to feel abundant, joyful, and free in the moment, and imagined living the life she wanted. Yet the structures of her beliefs still kept that experience from happening because the mind was competing with the beliefs that remained in the body and the corresponding energy systems, thereby creating resistance. When we moved the attention into the body though, to ask into the cellular structure and the emotions held in place there, she recognized that what resided there was actually running counter to what she wanted. It was familiar to her in a remote way. Through the wisdom of the body's insight, which was heard in the dialogue process, the client was shown a path to understand and release the body's counter intention. Once the mind and body were acting as one again, phenomenal change in her level of abundance occurred immediately. Just as water rushes forward when a boulder is removed from a river, life energy moves more directly and fully in all its beautiful forms when you resolve held patterns.

It was immensely satisfying for her to realize that she had everything she needed all along – all the information was stored right there inside her own body. The answers to her problems were literally right under her nose the whole time she was struggling. But there was no need for lamenting either, as the process brought other gifts that could not have been experienced otherwise. Since removing whatever was holding her back, she now experiences her personal power to create what she wants anew.

This is the essence of Spontaneous Transformation. We converse with the body to discover what we carry throughout our lives and how it shapes our reality. It is really a fun and miraculous process. Not all the Spontaneous Transformation sessions I do with clients follow the exact same steps in this precise order.

The next chapter, *Emotional Triggers and the Spontaneous Transformation,* explains each step in depth. As you read through actual sessions with clients and stories of my own in the following chapters using these steps, you will see the range of topics from which you can gain profound insight by using this one technique. You will also see how each one of these questions opens up a world of possibilities for the person answering them. Imagine what may be possible for you as you explore the powerful wisdom your body holds.

EMOTIONAL TRIGGERS and the SPONTANEOUS TRANSFORMATION

What is an Emotional Trigger?

A trigger is an event, circumstance, person, or thought that causes us to react or overreact emotionally. Anger, upset, jealousy, envy, whatever emotion you perceive as "bad," becomes a lower-vibrating frequency within your body. When somebody says something or something happens that makes you uncomfortable or upset, that's a trigger. It's also an opportunity to follow whatever got triggered, like a trail of breadcrumbs, inside to access the deeper part of you that is ready to understand it. Play with the trigger as if it is calling out to you in a game of hide-and-seek. Look around inside and ask, "What is the trigger I hold inside that instigates this uncomfortable emotion?"

Releasing Back Pain: My Story

There was a phase in my life when I experienced a great deal of back pain. I was afraid I'd become one of the millions of others who suffer from this common condition. Back pain is one of the most pervasive and debilitating ailments about which patients often complain. I knew it was rare to permanently relieve chronic back pain even when several options existed – from surgery to chiropractic to heating pads and every other remedy sold on late-night infomercials. So, when the back pain began to feel chronic, I began feeling pretty helpless and desperate. The condition was so uncomfortable, it limited me in practical ways and cost me time and money to address with no result. I was already using Spontaneous Transformation to remove emotional issues when they arose in my life, so I decided to use this same process to discover a new perspective on my physical source of discomfort.

I started with several deep breathing techniques just to get my mind into a place of stillness.

Then I went into my body and asked, "Okay, what exactly am I feeling right now?"

It was all too clear.

The body practically shouted, "I have a pain in my lower back!"

Next, I asked my body, "Where am I feeling this emotion/pain/ache?"

My attention immediately went to the lower, left-hand side where the pain was centered most of the time.

Keeping my focus inside this place in my back, as if I was sitting inside that lower, left back, I asked, "What does this feeling, or sensation, look like?"

As I observed the pain in my back, I noticed my colon felt heavy, but it also felt like it was moving and changing. This surprised me since it wasn't an issue of the muscles or vertebrae.

"What is this about?" I wondered. As I asked the pain in my back this question, I got the sense that it was turning its back on me as if responding with indifference.

I spoke directly to the part of my back that responded indifferently to me to let it know: "I am here, I am listening, and I am no longer ignoring you. What can I do for you?"

That same part melted into sadness and revealed that anger and frustration were just a front to hide the sadness.

I asked, "Why is this sadness here? How is it serving me?"

It told me that I am so much more than what I have allowed myself to show the outside world. It told me that every time I hold this sadness, instead of feeling it and releasing it, there will be pain and tension in my back. This pain is actually my barometer that lets me know whether I am living authentically in the world – or not – in that moment.

As I delved into why I was holding this sadness in my back, I found it was because I was teased and ferociously taunted during childhood.

So I asked my back, "What kind of a belief did this set up?"

What I heard was that I told myself, "It isn't safe to reveal my true self." That was the belief: that I risked love and acceptance if I showed all authentic parts of my nature.

So I asked, "What do you need?"

As I felt into my body, I discovered, "I need absolute self-love."

"What does it look like? Feel like? What is the sensation of self-love fully expressed?"

By going inward to feel self-love in that moment, I realized, I didn't have any template for self-love! I didn't have it available to me in that moment. I couldn't recall ever experiencing it.

So I asked into the body, "What is it to experience self-love?"

As I went more deeply inward and waited for the answer to come, my body showed me. It was such a miracle, I could only describe it as the sensation of the need expressed and fulfilled at the same time.

I asked again, "What does self-love feel like?" This time it felt like light opening my heart.

I asked again, "Okay, what does light opening my heart feel like?" And another level revealed itself like all possibilities are available.

"What does that feel like?" I ask.

"All possibilities available to me feels like peace." That was it. I dwelled there in that deep seat of peace, right where the pain had settled in order to bring my attention to what I could instead experience. The childhood hurt remained in my body as a lower energetic that got triggered so that I could bring love to it.

That beautiful moment of back pain led me to this feeling of what my soul had yearned for all along, and now I have it in my body. It's part of my being and my energetic infrastructure. This supports everything I do now in life. Love is something I have and can give to myself. I don't need to go out and try to get it from someone else. I have it to give whenever that part of me hurts and feels it is lacking my love. This is how we create a new energetic blueprint for something inside our soul to be expressed and become an integral part of us.

If you get overwhelmed by your issues, consider that resolving them is a bit like resistance training. The weight at the gym is not evil or bad. It is there to create just the resistance you need to develop your muscles. Working regularly with the resistance makes you healthier and stronger in the long run. Working to resolve your personal issues gives you inner-strength and the ability to thrive. Even the problems we are all facing now on a global scale will cause us to have to do things differently, face "our stuff" and find balance and more love for ourselves and others. Whenever my back pain starts to return again, I go through the same process, but each time at a much deeper level. I feel that peace reach into every cell in my body. I let love expand my heart beyond its seeming capacity. I lift that weight every day to feel it, to work that heart like the muscle that it is, so that it stays strong through anything and everything. What happens is, the fulfillment (that there really are no words for) expands and becomes part of who I am. That part of me becomes a piece of my expanded blueprint, or energetic signature.

For the next thirty days, allow yourself to feel that love. Grow that muscle. Most, if not all, traumas end up being a call for more love to be sent to the source. So, start there.

This first Spontaneous Transformation session begins with a guided process, which I call the Pearl Meditation. It moves you into a very quiet, still point within your body. I call this place, *the sacred chamber.* It is a place where love resides. Once there, you will feel more of your true self. When you start from this place feeling truth, your visualizations will be that much more powerful. It is the place inside from which you can create anything. You will know you have found it when you feel completely safe and at peace. As a caveat, know that having even just an inkling of safety and peace – even if it feels like a faraway sensation or vision – is the perfect start. You may not feel the deep sense of it at first, but whatever experience you are having, whether deep or very surface-like, is absolutely perfect.

Power, Beauty and Confidence: A Spontaneous Transformation

The following excerpt is from a monthly group conference call that I share three Saturdays each month with hundreds of callers from around the world at my online *MasterWorks Healing Membership Site*. The participant on this particular call, Sonia, called in with pain in her stomach and, after some examination, delved into the trauma she had been holding in that area.

There is always something that will assist you from another's experience. We are all part of the same web of existence, so it is no accident that you are reading this now – it is here for *you*. I suggest you let yourself experience the opening meditation exercise then, as Sonia moves into her own body's wisdom, you can delve into your own sensations to process any of your own issues by following my questions and suggestions.

I begin the Spontaneous Transformation Process with Sonia by saying, "Begin by imagining that there's a beautiful pearl hovering above your head. It is perfect, absolutely perfect, and it's emanating a really remarkable vibration and light, almost like an unworldly light. Picture that you are holding a magnifying glass and you are peering into the layers of this beautiful pearl.

"Really start to investigate and feel into the energy of the pearl. As you do this, you will sense the beautiful layers within. Each layer represents the perfect essence of love, joy, peace, abundance, health, and wholeness and all the essences of divine love."

The energy on the call relaxes into a silent sweetness, I continue, "Yes, that's it. As you witness this beauty before you, this beautiful, beautiful energy before you, each of these layers are vibrating at the level of frequency that is love and joy, peace and abundance, health and wholeness, and all other Divine qualities. These are the beautiful qualities that represent the purest energy. As you look at this and observe this and feel this, you are going to notice something really interesting!

"*This is actually you.* This is you. This is you at your core. This is your spark. This is the *you* that has always been there and always will be there. This pearl drops into your head, as if it was dropped in a still pool of water. Then it gently sinks within your head and body.

"This beautiful energy reminds each thing it passes of this resonant frequency of Divinity; the Divine energy that is you. It passes the pituitary and pineal glands. It gives these glands an energetic nudge, rekindling the feeling of pure love. It passes the sinus, reminding that beautiful sinus of the energy of pure love."

So often in life, we are too busy to even think about the amazing parts that make up the whole of our body, like our sinuses, our pituitary and thyroid glands, and our throat.

"That pure essence of love goes deeper and deeper… into the throat chakra and the thyroid. It reminds the thyroid and the throat chakra of pure love. The pearl swirls gently and slowly as it sinks within you. As if it has been dropped into a pool of water, ripples of light waft through your body all the way to your fingers and toes and then all the way back to your center, creating a ripple effect throughout your entire body. This perfect source energy is now emanating through the entire body and it goes out and out," as I held for about six to seven seconds making sure the rhythmatic breathing is rippling out, and in, out and in, like a cats purr or a sleeping baby.

I continue, "As the pearl passes the heart, it moves into the sacred chamber."

The special place of the sacred chamber, I identify, as a place behind and below the heart.

Continuing, "This beautiful sacred chamber is a place in which you enter and experience full source energy. This is your deepest connection to source. This is your deepest connection to you. As you move within that energy, you feel its gentle loving embrace. You feel the support that's there as the atmosphere changes into a place of stillness. Are you getting that, Sonia?"

From a state of relaxation and trust, Sonia replies, "Yes."

I continue, "As you feel that beautiful connection to the Divine, Sonia, you are filled up. This is where you know that you *know*. Do you understand me when I say that?"

Sonia replies, "Yes."

I move forward affirming, "Good. Now we are going to bring our attention into your body. We are going to move out of the sacred chamber and we are going to bring all this beautiful and supportive energy with us. So, you're surrounded with this beautiful sacred chamber energy, yet you are bringing your attention fully into the body.

"And we are going to ask the body, 'Body, where is the place in you that wants a voice, that wants to talk to Sonia?'

"Sonia, your body is calling to you. Where in your body do you feel your body talking to you? It might be a place of tension or a place of emotional holding. It might even be a place of pain. One place in particular is calling you. What part of your body is saying, 'Sonia, I need your attention?'"

Sonia immediately responds, "My stomach."

I affirm, "Good. Just bring your focused attention now to your stomach. What does it look or feel like there?"

Sonia follows intently, "My stomach feels big."

I push in on the point of focus asking, "Sonia, the stomach feels big?"

Sonia answers, "Yes."

I inquire, "What does it mean that the stomach feels big?"

Sonia describes, "My stomach feels bloated and just very thick, like a thick balloon."

"Thick like a balloon?" I ask knowing that we were making progress in the Spontaneous Transformation, "Is there any emotion that is coming with this thick, balloon-like feeling?"

"Maybe a bit of anger," as Sonia's voice stiffens, "anger with myself."

Knowing this process requires attentiveness, I ask, "How does this anger with yourself show up as a bloated, thick balloon?"

Sonia responds with uncertainty, "Jennifer, when you say, 'Show up,' what do you mean?"

"Great question," acknowledging Sonia, I answer, "Describe what the anger looks like in your stomach as it shows up within this bloated, thick balloon?"

"The feeling is very hard," Sonia reflects, "It feels like it doesn't belong there, like I don't know why it is there."

I tell Sonia to ask her stomach, "Why are you here?"

Sonia repeats to her stomach, "Why are you here?"

I ask, "What is the response?"

Sonia answers, "I knew right away what the answer was when I asked my stomach. I am angry about what happened. I think I feel guilty about feeling angry too."

Sonia has just brought in a secondary feeling into the picture.

I inquire further, "Sonia, can you tell me when the first time you had that feeling? Do you remember how old you were? Do you remember the first time you had that angry feeling?"

"I think what really pops up is when I was," Sonia stutters, "...I think I was thirteen."

Focusing the session further, I dig deeper, "Sonia, I'd like you to bring your attention to that thirteen-year-old. This powerful, beautiful woman that you are now, who is fully sensing and feeling your power within your sacred chamber, bring yourself fully into this beautiful moment of power and beauty and confidence. Bring that energy now to that thirteen-year-old, so that she can see you, sense you, feel you, and feel your support."

After a moment I ask, "How is she doing?"

Sonia responds smiling, "She's really well."

With delight, knowing an important connection had been made, I say, "She's pretty impressed, isn't she?"

Enthusiastically, Sonia says, "Yes, she is jumping around right now."

I reinforce the point of focus with Sonia by saying, "Good. Continue to see yourself there with her. I want her to feel completely supported and completely heard by you. So just imagine, have you had moments in your life when someone got you? Think of one moment. You had one moment in your life when someone really got you. That is the moment, your thirteen-year-old is having right now. What does it feel like for her to be gotten by you?

"Now, you are opening up space for her to share what is going on with her. She's going to show you what happened; she's going to share with you her guilt about feeling angry. All you are going to do is hold the space for her to empty her basket. You are going to listen to her."

It's quiet for a moment or two. Sonia carefully takes in what she has been hearing from me.

Finally Sonia begins to express, "I was sitting with my uncle and my mom. I was very, very quiet and introverted when I was young. My mom was quite overpowering. I felt very awkward and uncomfortable around other adults. My uncle, my mother's brother, just started talking with my mother, as if I wasn't even there. I was invisible. I didn't exist. I was unimportant. This made me really, really angry."

I listen with compassion and understanding.

"He thought there was something wrong with me," she continued unaware of how much energy she was releasing in recounting the story.

I make sure to acknowledge Sonia's feelings.

"I was so quiet." Sonia continues at a quickening pace, "He thought that I should get checked out because he thought there was something wrong with me like I was incapacitated.

"I remember sitting there and I was just thinking to myself, 'What an idiot he is.'"

Following Sonia's emotional energy as much as her words, I say, "Yes, let's bring your attention to that young teenage girl, okay? She just shared with you a beautiful and powerful story with us, so we are going to thank her for it. Let's make sure she knows that she has been heard fully and completely; furthermore, she needs to know that what happened, wasn't cool. It wasn't okay to be talked about as if she, or you as a young girl, were not there. It wasn't okay to be talked about as if there was something wrong with you. That was hurtful and painful. We are going to take a moment now and just acknowledge that for her. Let me know when you/ she are ready."

Sonia exhales slowly, like she's releasing a breath she's been holding in for a lifetime, and she finally says, "Yes."

Now I take Sonia into a process I call re-patterning.

I talk her through it by saying, "So, you are now coaching your teenage self, and you don't have to tell us what the coaching is per se. The words are unimportant, but you are sharing with her how she might have reacted in a way that was more empowering. You are giving her permission to play with this energy without making her feel right or wrong about any of it.

"So, let's bring her into a different world now. We have the real story of what happened, but we can also create a fantasy world of what could have happened. In this game of pretend, she now stands up in that moment, looks him right in the eyes, and she says what to him?"

Immediately Sonia responds on behalf of her thirteen year old girl, "Are you an idiot?"

I ask, "Did he or didn't he hear her now?"

Sonia answers, "Yes, he heard it loud and clear."

"Is there anything else that she would like to say to him?" I ask Sonia, "State his name, too."

With command, Sonia says, "Uncle Neil, that hurt my feelings, and I am standing right here. I am shy because I am an observer, but this doesn't make me bad or wrong. I don't speak because I am watching and witnessing. I am taking all of this in, and I know exactly what is going on. I am not stupid; in fact, I know I am very smart.

"When I am ready, I will speak. What you said about me was very disrespectful, and I am not okay with it. This is my moment of speaking, can you hear me?"

Impressed, I ask, "And what does he say?"

He answers Sonia with, "I can hear you."

I ask Sonia about her thirteen-year-old, "What does it feel like for her to be heard by her Uncle Neil?"

"It feels good," answers Sonia with gratification, "I kind of feel a release from him, too. He was genuinely concerned, something I didn't realize about him until now."

"Good," I say.

I like it when my clients have this type of recognition. I like it when they can put themselves in the other person's shoes and gain a new perspective about the situation that they had not previously accessed.

Moving forward with the exercise, I ask Sonia, "After you, at thirteen-years-old, stood up to your uncle, what happens to this girl when she goes back to school? Is there a shift you can talk about? Are things different when she has her first date? Becomes a young woman? How can this energy show up differently now?"

Sonia responds thoughtfully, "A lot more confident."

This is the importance of the re-patterning process in the Spontaneous Transformation. Sonia accessed a sense of confidence that allowed her to see situational change in her past that created a new vibrational resonance. By re-patterning this experience, Sonia tapped into the power of her inner voice, she shifted the perspective she's held onto from her past, and she embraced an internal power that's been locked up inside her gut.

I ask her, "What does it feels like right now in your stomach?"

"It feels smaller," a relieved Sonia answers.

I follow up with asking, "Let's bring your attention back to your stomach and ask your stomach if there is anything else that is needed here?"

"I think I forgive myself," with some sense of certainty, Sonia responds.

"What does that look like for you, Sonia?" I ask.

"I need to put myself first. I need to speak up for myself," answers Sonia.

"And moving forward, how will this show up in your life?" I ask.

"I will take care of myself. I will get healthier. I will eat better. I will work out," Sonia says with hope and confidence for a positive future self. "I can see now that all the stuff that I've been neglecting even though my background is in health professionally, but I was behaving locked up in myself."

"I agree," I state, "Once again, the cobbler's children has no shoes. You are the leader, the health care provider, who's not taking care of herself. I believe the new, improved version of yourself wants to be an authentic leader that will share what is going on for you as a model of health and wellness to others. Is that true?"

"Yes," Sonia concedes.

I remind Sonia by saying, "You get to be a Divine being having a human experience. You don't have to be perfect to be the example. You get to lead by example, by being someone who is having a real life event show that you can resolve, realign, and re-pattern and that, my friend, is Spontaneous Transformation."

Getting the Learning

Sonia discovered that she already knew why she was holding what she was holding. Sonia lost a lot of additional weight she was holding after our session. This tied into both the emotional past she was holding onto, and the now self that wasn't taking care of herself. She went onto be a model of health and wellness, and, today, has a flourishing practice.

This is always true about the body – when we ask into the body, it always answers with the truth. And it is ready to relinquish what it has been holding onto when we are willing to take the time to ask and get the learning.

The body is a teacher that holds out the root cause of our pain, or anger, or hurt, etc., as a gift – the opportunity to grow and expand beyond it, that is the greater purpose of pain. The beauty of Spontaneous Transformation is that you have that opportunity to transform pain the moment you are willing to look at it. Like Sonia, you have the answers you need within yourself that will allow you to release the internally imprinted pattern.

Now it's time to try out this process on yourself.

The 7-Step Spontaneous Transformation: Practice

STEP #1: Acknowledge your current triggered emotion in the moment. Use it to discover a new perspective. Ask: *What am I feeling right now?*

The Spontaneous Transformation process begins with recognizing our emotions, particularly the challenging emotions, like fear, depression, and anger. Think of a situation that you would like to be different, or one that constantly upsets you, or a chronic physical condition that you would prefer not to have. Instead of trying to deny these feelings, utilize them as an access point into the body, and into a loving relationship with yourself. It begins by placing your attention and awareness inside the body to simply listen. This is the acknowledgment that it has something of value to communicate to you. Someone just cut you off on the highway and a part of you is going, "That just pisses me off!" This is a great example of a trigger because we can all relate to it. Here's your chance to gain a new perspective. Rather than just sit there railing against someone else, bring your awareness to the emotion. Acknowledge the moment, whatever it is: "I'm really upset," or "I'm so sad" or "I'm hurt, or disappointed, or confused, helpless, angry, or worried…"

The essence of Spontaneous Transformation is noticing where you are in every moment, but the tool is especially powerful when you're triggered. An emotional trigger has been pulled today or in the moment. Something happened and now the feeling of (fill in the blank) just won't go away. It's immediate, it's compelling, and it's pulling you into a conversation because it has something to show you. Like a child who whispers, "I have something I want to tell you," if you don't listen at first, or you continue to ignore it, it will begin to shout loudly. It will repeat itself until it gets your complete attention. So you best pay attention now, before it resorts to pain. Get present. Get yourself into a listening place where you can clearly hear the answer to the following six questions.

STEP #2: Move your focus and attention inward. Ask: *Where am I feeling this emotion/pain/ache in my body?*

Is there a place in my body that's holding this emotion more strongly than others? Just ask and your body will direct your attention to where it lies. Remember: it's just an exploration. Begin the journey with immense curiosity. No need for trepidation. You're safe. Once you are present to your experience, you may be surprised where it is being held. The more obvious areas where many of us hold pain or stiffness is in the neck or back. It might, however, be somewhere completely different. Perhaps in the calf, in the stomach, or even in the heart. Feel into the body. It will guide you and take you to the exact point of feeling the emotion or sensation. Trust the body's communication.

STEP #3: Move your attention to that specific body part or area.

Go there now. Shift into that area as if you are inside your body so that you can look around you. Share with this body part, "I'm present. I'm listening. I am moving my attention to this part of my body now. I'm not going anywhere. I'm here now." Say it several times. We are not used to being present with ourselves. We avoid discomfort and things we don't yet understand. Be gentle, curious, willing. Bring your full attention to the body now because in the past, we have ignored it. We may have abandoned certain aspects of ourselves and cut off communication, so it's important to really go there and know it's real.

STEP #4a: Arrive in that place. Look around. Sense what is there. Describe it to yourself in detail. Ask: *What is the feeling? What is the sensation? What does this look like?*

For those people who are very visual, as you bring your attention to that part of your body, you might see an image there, like a rock or a clenched fist or someone's face. Everyone has their own representations. My clients have seen armor, knives, a sword, a ball of wire, a color, some of which have had particular significance and associations to their past. Others who are not as visual often experience a sensation there, like a twinge, or a tingling, a tightness, heat or cold. Others describe the feelings there. For example, when my attention is focused on the point of pain in my back, it looks black and uninviting. It feels angry and indifferent at the same time. I see a mixture of red and black.

Observe whatever is present. Without judgment or trying to figure it out, watch and feel what comes up. Throughout my therapeutic practices, I have discovered that just by observing our sensation, there is an opportunity for it to shift. I call this the "Observer Effect." By just simply observing, the body says, "Oh my God, you're here. You're really here. You're present. You're hearing. You're listening. You're observing! Thank you! This is what we have been waiting for." Whatever has been buried is now revealed. The body offers it up. That, alone, can create a huge energy shift.

Please note: *If you are seeking a quick exploratory session that will move you forward, go directly from Step 4a to Step 5. If you are seeking a deeper session to further resolve the issue, then read on to Step 4b. This step is optional. It represents the advanced work of comprehensive life issues.*

STEP #4b: To apply the advanced Spontaneous Transformation process: Ask: *What is this about? What kind of a belief did this set up?*

This is where you have the chance to begin dialoguing with the deeper emotional and spiritual components of any memories attached to the image or sensation. The advanced work goes deeper within this area of the body to gain insight into larger issues that affect significant areas of your life. You don't have to address this aspect of your experience every time a trigger arises and you enter into Spontaneous Transformation.

This step can bring you back into the trauma in such a profound way that it can re-traumatize the system. In the eighties, when this was a grand experiment, we went into "what happened." Now, it is no longer necessary nor recommended to subject your body to the past trauma by re-experiencing it. You need only acknowledge what happened and perhaps observe it from a safe, loving place inside. Once you've gone through the whole book and seen where the process can take you, you will be more prepared to go back and use this Step 4b.

The sensation that shows up is generally symbolic and representative of a larger issue. Like a weed, you need to get at its roots if you really want to remove it once and for all. Otherwise, it will keep coming back or growing bigger and taking over a larger area of your inner garden. If you want to probe into the root cause of the sensation or image you received, then ask your body directly, "What is this about?"

Usually you will get an answer like, "When I was two, this happened to me. When I was five, this happened to me." This moment can provide a real revelation. It adds up and the answer leaves us feeling like, "I get it! That's what this was about all this time!"

You may get a repressed memory that you have never thought about prior to this dialogue. It can be a well-remembered moment, but now it offers a new bit of information. Maybe you suddenly see the same memory with its corresponding emotional subtext or you get a revelation about the other person or people involved.

This is when you can ask the body, "What kind of a belief did this set up?"

In this phase of dialoguing, you can explore, "What really happened here? Which thoughts did I have in that moment that imbued that situation with meaning?" Beyond the experience itself, you created an interpretation and a perception of yourself, others and perhaps the nature of the life you would experience from then on. You could be amazed at some of the answers you get such as, "Well, I thought that in order to protect myself, I had to hurt myself," "I figured that being loved was the same as being abandoned," or, "I knew, in that moment, I wasn't worthy of love unless I was perfect."

Often when we experience a trauma in our early development, a fallacious belief system is internalized. My therapeutic experience has revealed that most of our false belief systems and adult trauma can be linked back to seeds that were planted in childhood. Those seeds grow into the same issue playing itself out in intimate relationships, professional environments, etc. At this level of revelation, the idea of you creating your own reality begins to make sense. Often this out-picturing of the past in the present is more easily recognized in others rather than the self. If you have ever observed a loved one over the years as they create and recreate the same types of challenges, you can recognize how that pattern then forms the fabric of their lives. You cannot know what their learning experience represents for them. Only they can eventually discover this. It is, again, for you to be present with your own patterns and choose when you would like to finally gain understanding from them and bring love to those aspects of yourself that you can transform them forever.

STEP #5: Ask that body part: *What do you need?*

From Step 4a, feeling into the body part that is "holding," you will know if it is enough to ask the sensation, image or feeling, "What do you need?" The body most often gives us soul answers that are Divine in nature like,

"I need acceptance. I need support. I need acknowledgement. I need love." The body does not give us shaming answers such as: "I need for you to lose ninety pounds." That's your critical mind talking. The body does not give you "should" directives. The body gives you "affirming" directives. As you use the Spontaneous Transformation, you will recognize how your body expresses its needs. It will always be something that you have to give.

STEP #6: Give the body what it needs by asking: *What would it feel like to experience that need as fully expressed? What does that look like? What is the experience or sensation of that need being fulfilled? How would you like to experience this?*

Use the words "look" if you are more visual; "feel" if you more easily access feelings; and "sensation or experience" if you relate better to that, as most men do. Customize the question to what is right for you. After you get an answer as to what you need, the key here is to actually create within yourself the body's affirming directive. The first part of the question is asked to that particular aspect of the body or body part. It knows how to show you the sensation of that need expressed as an aspect of the mastery of you into which you are tapping at this moment. Essentially, you are asking, "In what form or how does the body need it?" Well, let's see. What does love look and feel like? Often, it feels or looks like a form of energy: A warmth in that area of the body; a sensation of the heart expanding; extremities tingling; a glowing light; a sense of peace; a feeling of being held in support.

A step that may come up naturally is the body offering a quality that could be expressed and experienced in life on a more consistent basis. In other words, it might offer ideas on how you can you continue to give yourself what you need. Your body may want love in the form of healthy habits or saying nice, supportive things to yourself every morning to start the day, or finally pursuing a long-buried dream and desire to sing or just taking time out of your busy schedule for yourself to relax and do nothing. Your body may give you a specific answer like, "I need to go for a walk every morning." These are self-nurturing acts that continue to strengthen your relationship with your body and support yourself to re-pattern the way you do life and think about yourself.

While these self-nurturing suggestions may come up time to time, the real juice is the "need expressed;" playing with the energy which answers the "what do you need" question. This is the foundational energy that the soul requires to obtain health, wellness, alignment, balance, safety and love.

Each of us will come to our own conclusion of what love, or support, or acknowledgment looks and feels like to us. Just keep asking, "What does this look and feel like?" until you tap into a core energy. When you get to that core energy, you will recognize it because your body will feel as if it has just expanded outwards and opened up. When you reach that point, you will know.

STEP #7: Try to feel or sense the initial triggered emotion. It will have changed if not disappeared, and the body part will feel better, too.

This is a simple checking-in with self. The triggered emotion is almost certainly gone. If it is still there in any form, it is worth going back through the steps in a more dedicated way. This step affirms an ongoing conversation and willingness to stay present and listen to the body. As long as you are giving it what it needs, it will let you know all is well. This is not to say that other triggers might not ignite other issues, or that this particular physical/emotional component will not arise in other forms triggered by other events. It may even remain a theme throughout your life. Now you have a way to learn what you need from it. As you continue being receptive and fulfill its needs the best you can, the pattern or theme will diminish, moving further and further away from your core and further outside of your energy field of experience.

MOVING FEAR and the CRITICAL VOICE OUTSIDE YOUR ENERGY FIELD

A woman called into the *MasterWorks Healing Membership Site* with a determined voice asking, "How do I embrace fear?" That was an excellent question. Embracing our fear is a noble notion; however, it's like asking how to embrace fire. We are not meant to stick our hands in a campfire and scoop up an armful of burning logs and give them a bear hug. This would sear our flesh, and the heat is a natural deterrent that reminds us to avoid it. You don't have to embrace fear. It's scary and overwhelming and that is why we shy away from it.

Yet, life circumstances continue to present opportunities to deal with the experience of fear. Perhaps we find ourselves with mounting bills and shrinking bank accounts. Or we wake up and the first thought that comes to mind is, "How will I cope when I feel overwhelmed by so many problems?"

It seems that every day is fraught with heavy burdens and risky, weighty decisions. Even as a global community, we are confronted by frightful events in the news and people whose sole purpose is to arouse terror in others. It has become a very important question: "What do we do with fear? What can we learn from it? How can we use it to move forward?"

How to Use Fear

The way we too often approach life is to develop a new companion called fear, which we keep by our side from the moment we wake up in the morning. Even in sleep, some get no reprieve from fearful thoughts and dreams. Fear becomes something like an angry, stray dog circling at our feet, barking and yapping the dreadful, catastrophic worse case scenarios.

How are we to treat this constant companion called fear?

Our ego, working in a kind of partnership with the mind, is actually meant to utilize fear as a warning signal. The ego is so often referred to as a bad thing, and even the root of our problems. Actually, both the ego and the mind play integral roles in the process of keeping our bodies healthy and whole. Our ego helps hold the structure of our personality in place so that we maintain functioning in the world. The mind interacts and interfaces with the ego to make its own choices. When a person is working only from the mind, the mind has to make decisions that it is not fully equipped to make. When someone is in the body and being guided from a heart space, the heart allows intention to manifest. The mind is then best used, enthusiastically supplying us with intellect, so the heart can be guided into right decisions. The mind is a beautiful partner. Our mind can recognize that there is a cliff up ahead and yell at us, "Danger! Stop!" This is how fear plays a vital role in keeping us safe.

Twenty-nine climbers once scaled K2, which is the second highest mountain in the world after Mount Everest. Its peak is steeper, and covered in sheer ice. These climbers were some of the best climbers in the world. When they had almost reached the summit, several of them were too exhausted to continue, so only a few went on to scale the peak and view the sun setting over the valley. As they descended the crest of the mountain, the ice cracked, cascading down and sweeping away some of those who waited below. The survivors were left to descend back to base camp in the dark without safety ropes. Unbelievably, a few of these climbers managed this insane feat and made it back down the mountain. Did they experience fear?

Undoubtedly. Their hyper-awareness of the risk factor kept them focused on the task in front of them. They accomplished their goal with a combination of skill, intention and resolve.

In desperate situations in life, we seem to be given the insurmountable task of blindly groping our way through treacherous conditions. We can use the fear to motivate us to move even when we think we can't. For this, we need resolve, intention and skill to push beyond the sense of overwhelm. We get this by having an inroad into that place of deep knowing which speaks louder than fear. If we don't believe that there is at least a chance to make it successfully, how would we overcome our life challenges?

Resolve and intention come from self-belief: however small, the inkling that says, "I can make it" must exist somewhere inside. If you cannot hear that voice, there may be a critical voice there instead sending you the message that you don't have what it takes to make it. That's an indicator that you need to find your own authentic voice within and listen to it. The true voice inside knows you because it is you. Even when all evidence suggests otherwise, it can guide you to overcome any challenges you are facing.

There is a way to set that critical voice aside and tune into a deeper knowing. When you are intent on listening to that deeper truth, fear subsides.

Attuning your ear and your heart to that still, small voice within is a vital skill. You have to listen long and hard enough to recognize its wisdom and guidance beyond the fear. It takes practice. You know that old joke… a guy walking in New York City asks another carrying a violin case, "How do you get to Carnegie Hall?" The guy answers, "Practice, practice, practice." It's true. That is what it takes. Vigilant, consistent, daily practice to listen to your truth, to use moments of triggered emotions to pay attention to your needs, to practice self-forgiveness, and even practice listening to fear so that you can make life choices from a place of awareness and inner knowing.

It is important to recognize, though, that there are different types of fear. There is the type of fear that debilitates and stops us in our tracks; then there is the type of fear that motivates us to move us forward.

The Fear that Holds Us Back

When we are grappling with a fear that cripples us, or renders us inert, we do not need to embrace this type of fear. Nor should we run from this type of fear. Instead, we can respect it and acknowledge it. We pay attention to this fear and address it by listening, moving within, and moving it outside of our energy field. Listening to the body's truth will help you discern between the fear that debilitates and the fear that motivates.

When we come to an understanding of why the fear is present, we can transform it and release it when appropriate.

Debilitating fear is like an impenetrable wall of fire that stops us in our tracks. We believe that we can't walk through it without getting burned. Our ego uses this type of fear and screams, "I can't move forward because what if this horrible thing happens, or what if this other horrible thing happens?"

If we let this type of fear get a foothold inside us, it will take on a life of its own and become the insidious, shrill voice of panic or chronic worry within, like that voice yapping away about what *could* happen while barking orders for you to be careful and avoid this and that. That type of fear eats away at our determination and self-belief. Without hope, forward movement seems pointless. We find we are stuck, afraid to make a move in any direction.

I often use a technique with my clients who are debilitated by fear called, "Catastrophizing." This is when I actually have my clients use their imagination to take their worst fears to the nth degree so that they can finally concretize what they are actually so scared about. Here's an example.

A woman claimed that she could not possibly leave her job, one that she hated, because she was afraid.

I simply asked, "What is the very worst that would happen? What is the catastrophe that would inevitably ensue based on that one decision?"

"Well, I'd be homeless in a month," she said.

I have found in asking this simple question that homelessness is often the fear which is imagined as the worst thing in the world that could possibly happen to anyone. This fear causes people to *not* pursue a more fulfilling career or relationship.

Instead of trying to convince her that this wouldn't happen, I said, "Okay, let's go there. What would happen then?" Usually people haven't thought beyond that because being homeless seems like the last stop in a string of catastrophes. So, when they try to imagine what could be worse, what happens is that they always take the scenario all the way to the end... everyone goes to death. We have fear of death *and* of life. They invariably see how futile it is to refuse to live the life they want as a way of avoiding death. As soon as they can lose the fear of death, life becomes easier. Choices become simpler. They are not catastrophizing the consequences of every small decision. They are freer to pursue life.

The kicker here, is that a majority of the time, the horrible thing that we imagine *might* happen, will never happen. Yet, the fear of what might happen keeps us stuck. Even if something remotely similar did happen, in the end, we would still be fine no matter what. Think of a time in your life when you thought of the worst-case scenario, and aspects of that scenario came true... are you still alive? For some, you may even be thriving. You came through it, in some cases with flying colors, and stronger than before. This is the evidence you can actually use in moments of fear to remember – YOU WILL BE FINE.

Releasing fear – and the critical voice that says you can't manage it – may need to be a regular practice for you. The more you release unnecessary fear, the more familiar it will become to live without it. Here is a Spontaneous Transformation practice that will allow you to walk through that wall of fire to stand on the other side of fear.

Release Fear: Practice

Spontaneous Transformation can be used to place your fear, and that doubting, fretful voice that doesn't actually belong to you, outside of your energy system. This will allow you to explore what your body feels like when you are not holding this crippling emotion. Now is the best time to start this practice. You don't know all the wonderful opportunities your fear is preventing you from experiencing right now.

1) *Get familiar with the fear you carry concerning a certain situation or person.*

Start by bringing your attention into your body. Tap on your heart with your fingertips and take a couple of nice, deep breaths as you do that. Breathe in and out through your nose. Imagine sucking the air through your heart, then release the air out your mouth. Bring your attention into this moment, into your heart. As you relax, I want you to remember something that makes you feel some degree of fear, while at the same time knowing in this moment that you are completely safe. In this moment, you are fine. You are supported by your soul, by the Divine.

Now, feel the fear that is within you somewhere. It has its own associations. "What does that fear look, feel or sound like within you, right now?" It might take on a personality. It might actually be representative of someone else's fear, so you may hear it as the voice of a parent, a relative, a teacher, a friend, or someone who caused some trauma for you. Your fear could also appear as an object. Or it could just be a tactile sense.

Now that you know what the fear looks, feels or sounds like, ask your mind, "Mind, is it okay if we play with this energy right now? This fear may come back fully intact later if it serves me. But for now, I just want to explore it."

If the mind is resistant, then find out, "What does my mind need to allow me to play with fear for a moment?" Allow that in. Honor what your mind has requested. It could be that your mind needs to rest, which seems to happen a lot when we deal with fear because overwhelm can be exhausting. If that's the case, let the mind rest. Reassure your mind that everything is safe and okay, and we're just going to play here.

With its consent, feel that fear within you now. What does it look like? What does it feel like? What is the sense of it? Does it seem to be someone else's fear that was given to you over time?

2) *Place that fear outside of your energy field and describe how that feels.*

Let it know very clearly, "Fear, I would like you to move outside the boundary of my energy field now. Not just to the periphery of my awareness, but actually outside of my energy field." Imagine that your body exists within a field of energy, which extends beyond you and outward in all directions. Get a sense of how far-reaching it is so that you can know when the fear is set just outside of its parameters. It could be a few feet, twenty yards or several blocks. As we feel that fear moving to the outside, we can tell the fear that it can come back later. If it needs to, the fear will come back, when we are done with this exercise. That's okay. At least you will grow familiar for a time with the feeling of relieving your body of this uncomfortable energy of fear.

Now, feel that fear sitting outside of your energy field. Sense what it feels like in your body without that energy, without that system of fear, or without that fearful voice. What does it feel like in your body? Describe it to yourself. For example, "With the fear sitting outside, my body feels stronger. It feels more integrated. This feels good to me. It feels like a moment of infinite possibilities."

3) *Get familiar with who you are and how you feel WITHOUT the fear.*

Now, ask yourself this question, "What can I be? How can I show up in my life without this fear?" From this new place, can you feel the infinite possibilities? Can you imagine living your life without fear? Does it feel familiar at all? Was there ever a time you felt this way and everything was okay? Was it actually great?

Stay in this feeling for as long as you possibly can. This is more resistance training. You are working your peace muscle to develop your ability to stay in this new place so to not always revert to fear as a default protection mechanism. Practice living without the kind of fear that holds you back. Notice the happenings that affirm you can do life this new way.

When the fear is outside of your body, in this moment, all is possible. You are in flow. Do you know what happens when our energy is flowing unencumbered by fear? Everything is possible.

Transforming Fear: A Spontaneous Tranformation

In the following session from the *MastersWorks Healing Membership Site*, a participant named Barbara was experiencing tremendous fear around financial issues. We walked through the Spontaneous Transformation process together so that she could find freedom from this debilitating emotion, which kept her exactly where she didn't want to be. We placed her fear outside of her energy field so that she could grow familiar with how it felt to be without fear and to recognize other possibilities for her life. Follow along with her experience and apply my questions to any area of fear that might arise in you.

"I feel like I've made a huge mistake with my mother's investments," says an anxious Barbara. "She has Alzheimer's, and I am responsible for investing her money."

Listening, I respond, "Okay. Would you be willing to cycle through this pretty fast using Spontaneous Transformation?"

With a slight hesitation, Barbara agrees, but she is at a place where she is willing.

As you notice by now, Spontaneous Transformation needs to start by having the participant identify with their body.

I ask Barbara, "Do you have your body's permission to check in and scan for fear?"

Barbara is still unsure.

I ask, "Something doesn't feel okay. Can you tell me in this moment what is happening?"

Barbara grimaces and responds, "I'm feeling a little indigestion right now."

"Thank you," I say to Barbara. "This is good. Does your body want to participate?"

"I think I feel some resistance," admits Barbara. "I felt some resistance to leaving fear as I believe I actually treasure it."

In listening to Barbara's response I immediately pick up on one of her challenges. She says she, "Thinks she feels some resistance." Thinking is a mental activity of the mind and feeling is either emotional energy or physical energy. I follow along to see if she can feel into her body without the interference of her mind.

I inquire with her, "Barbara, where are you feeling this in your body?"

Barbara responds, "Diaphragm."

Guiding her attention to the diaphragm, I ask her to describe the feeling.

"It's hard like a board," even her voice constricts when she answers.

"Hard like a board," I repeat. "Good for noticing and giving voice. When the diaphragm is hard like a board, it is challenging to do just about anything. This is because the diaphragm is how we breathe. It is the mechanism through which breath of life flows. If we can't breathe, we can't bring in that nutrition and oxygen. If there's no oxygen, we can't think. We've got this hard-like-a-board diaphragm. Can you tell me if there is any color, feeling sense, temperature, or anything that goes along with that?"

"Right now, I'm feeling a shortness of breath," as Barbara's breathing quickens.

"Focusing into the hard-like-a-board, can't breathe space in your diaphragm, tell me the first thing that comes into your mind as I say, 'What is this about?'"

Immediately, "Fear," proclaims Barbara. "Fear of the future, fear of making mistakes, fear of being trapped in a job that's unfulfilling, fear of being myself."

As a life coach, healer, and transformational expert, when someone declares fear, they often don't realize that this is the core ingredient in which they are creating their own reality. When there is fear of the future, fear of making mistakes, fear of being trapped in an unfulfilling job, and fear of being one's self, that creates the vibrational resonance in the world. It's no wonder Barbara is scared she's ruining her mother's investments. She probably is, if she is running this program of fear as the creational ingredient in her reality.

Fear creates a repetitive cycle of more fear.

As I continue guiding Barbara through the Spontaneous Transformation process, I ask, "Can you put the fear into a little box? Imagining that we are going to take that laundry list of fears that you expressed in the hard-like-a-board place, and just put them aside for a moment into a box of your choice. We are moving the fear outside of your energy system."

There is silence while Barbara takes a moment for herself to move her fear into a little box.

"What does it feel like to have placed all of your fear outside of your energy field by placing fear in a little box? Does your body feel different?" I ask.

Exhaling, Barbara responds, "Much better… I'm taking a deeper breath."

Following up, I ask, "Barbara, can you describe now what it feels like in your life to have all of the fear in this little box outside of your own energy field?"

"Well, relaxed," responds Barbara, "and my future seems brighter."

Pushing forward I question, "What kind of job are you going to get when you are in this mode?"

Barbara shrinks back and says, "I'm tightening up a little bit."

As fear creeps back into Barbara's diaphragm based on the projection of the outcome to the question, fear is a recognizable familiar feeling.

The feeling of not having fear is unfamiliar. When someone is given the opportunity to open up energy to a new experience, the booby trap then becomes the fear of change. However, it has to shift because open energy vibrates at a new level, resonating with new and different things.

I ask calmly, "Barbara, can you take the new space that is tightening up and invite that to be put into the little box outside of your energy field? You may also check in with yourself to see if there is anything else that needs to be put into this box."

Barbara responds, "I do this sort of work with myself. I'll go for days or weeks feeling positive and optimistic. Then, all of a sudden, something will trigger me into the fear again."

"No one is immune to triggers," I interject, "And you know what, Barbara? You know what that's called? It's called life. It's called living your life. I get triggered every day, and I simply use it. I'm like, 'Okay, this is showing up because I'm ready to go a little deeper.'

"Instead of saying, 'God, I was feeling so good and now I'm not!' We say something like, 'Oh, here's something else that's showing up that's allowing me to take this new feeling even deeper.'

"When it's a moment of extreme fear, fit it in the box or adjust the box to fit the fear. When it's in a moment of, 'I can handle this fear, but I don't like it,' allow it to guide you. Do some Spontaneous Transformation, or do Byron Katie's, The Work, or do Mary A. Hall's Heart Thoughts or do the Sedona Method, or do EFT or do Ho'oponopono. These clearing techniques are for the moments, which are inevitable, when we are triggered. The minute you stop having those moments is the minute that you're going to walk on water."

Barbara humorously responds, "I've been waiting for that moment."

"We're not here to walk on water. We're here to experience the patterns that we choose to experience. This is our playground. Instead of resisting a trigger, and blocking the flow, we approach the trigger with curiosity asking ourselves what can we learn from this trigger?"

"So be kind to myself," recognized Barbara.

For Barbara to recognize that fear as a trigger is an indicator for herself to actually be kind to herself, may seem like a small breakthrough, but it's actually the breakthrough that comes from Spontaneous Transformation. By recognizing that she isn't bad or wrong because she's been triggered, allows her the breath she needs to approach the fear as an opportunity to gain information about herself and/or the situation in front her.

Interestingly enough, the shift to "be kind to herself" is a thought that will allow her body to relax; therefore, Barbara should not continue to have a restricted diaphragm. This new process will take time to replace the knee jerk reaction that Barbara has been having of reacting with habituated fear.

Overcome Overwhelm: Practice

I like to use this next practice when I feel especially stressed out from overwhelm, when worry creeps in or starts yelling in my ear, "I can't do everything! I want to do this, this, this and this! And I need to do this, this and this…I don't have the time I need!"

When I become aware of the bit of anxiety that is being created for myself, I instead change my thoughts to, "Wouldn't it be nice if I felt completely confident, knowing everything that needs to be taken care of is taken care of? Wouldn't it be nice if I could serve the people who need my guidance the most? Wouldn't it be nice if I just enjoyed what I can do in this moment?"

This calms me down every time, allowing me to simply do what I am here to do, which is to serve, not to worry.

This simple practice is yet another way to have a dialogue with yourself to mitigate overwhelm or anxiety or low-grade fear. Because our thoughts and our words create our emotional states, we can use them to generate fear, or to generate possibilities and solutions to the challenges we are facing. It does not deny or belittle the "problem." It moves us to a place to best deal with it.

Mary A. Hall, a healer and abundance coach, who is a contributor to the *MasterWorks Healing Membership Site,* uses the following technique with her clients with amazing results. She suggests that when we find ourselves imagining fearful consequences, using the simple phrase, "Wouldn't it be nice if…"

Then, instead of thinking of the worst-case scenario, think of a positive outcome that could occur. For example, "Wouldn't it be nice if I got that job I wanted? Wouldn't it be nice if I then doubled my income? Wouldn't it be nice if I lived in that house by the beach that I love?"

This process changes your energy immediately because it opens your mind to your options and keeps it focused on what you really want to create for yourself. It effectively distracts you from your tendency to imagine all the things you don't want to have happen, which generates a state of chronic fear, so that you can dwell in more positive feelings. Your life then changes to match your new energy.

1) *Become aware of the situation and the thoughts that are making you feel overwhelmed or fearful.*

Pay attention to the chronic thoughts and images that are filling your body with dread, fear and stress. "I'm so busy. I have to do everything on my own. I can't do it all. Everyone expects too much from me. But I have to deliver or else… I could lose my job!" Yikes! No wonder this person is walking around in overwhelm.

2) *Replace that thought of what you DON'T want with multiple examples of what you do want.*

Replace the fearful future scenario with its positive alternative. This is where intention, resolve and consistent practice come in. What is it you want? Instead of focusing on the "bad," focus on the possibilities you would prefer. If you feel tied to your job and your schedule, you might desire more freedom, for example. So you would say, "I want to feel free. Oh, and happy, too, instead of scared all the time. I want to feel confident. And taken care of… and have a different job!" Just start to play with all the alternatives that would be so much better than your experience now!

Remember, this isn't to deny your current situation with affirmations or wishful thinking. It's giving you space and reprieve to spend some time in possibility, thinking and creative imagination.

3) *Say "Wouldn't it be nice if..." and feel every experience you imagine.*

This phrase expands the energy and places your desire into the realm of the possible. Notice the shift in energy as you make up your own wonderful "Wouldn't it be nice if..." ideas.

Say them aloud! For example, the person in the above scenario might say: "Wouldn't it be nice if... I had more free time to travel with my family? Wouldn't it be nice if... my partner came home with that special meal that I love? Wouldn't it be nice if... my bank account were full of money from doing work I enjoy?"

This person could also think about how freedom and confidence could even show up in her current situation in new and interesting ways: "Wouldn't it be nice if... freedom showed up in my job? (Feel that.) Wouldn't it be nice if... freedom showed up now in my relationship? (Feel that.) Wouldn't it be nice if... confidence and serenity showed up in little ways and moments every day with a certain grace and ease?" You have just changed your energy by imagining what you want.

4) *Stay riveted on these wonderful possibilities.*

Again, you want to prolong this new energetic as long as you can. Allow your vivid imagination to keep you focused on all these wonderful experiences that are now available to you. Feel into your body as it experiences these accomplishments coming to fruition as if in the present moment. Maintain that new experience in your body so that it acclimates and accepts it as the new norm. You are not only giving yourself reprieve from the grip of negativity and fear, you are strengthening your serenity muscle, or excitement muscle, or whatever you desire instead. You can continue to experience this new truth in your probable future.

Coping in Desperate Circumstances: A Spontaneous Transformation

The next participant, Iris, who called into the *MasterWorks Healing Membership Site,* was going through a divorce. As if that were not enough, she was also in the process of losing her house and business, and suffering from a lot of self-doubt about her ability to change anything in her life. In the following session, Iris and I worked through how to deal with the plaguing doubt that can come with facing the unknown. As Iris describes her experience, fill in your own experience. You don't have to be going down the same road as Iris to find this incredibly effective. Many people who have participated in my group coaching sessions tell me that they have deep releases through being present for the transformation of someone else.

"Jennifer, my concern is that sometimes when I am trying to work with the law of attraction, I find myself barraged by negative thoughts, like 'I'm not going to be able to find a job.' Or 'I'm not going to be able to find an apartment' and so on. So, I hear myself say that and then I say, 'Okay, let's change that.' But when I start saying, 'Yes, I will find a job. Yes, I will find an apartment,' it becomes this constant back and forth. I feel like it's a war."

As Barbara pointed out the opportunity that fear had for us, Iris is pointing out doubt. I often witness doubt as a belief, or a trauma, that is in your subconscious.

True to form, Iris says, "I doubt this is going to work for me."

As we begin another Spontaneous Transformation, I say to Iris, "The opportunity here is to clear the doubt. Don't repress it. Don't deny it because, if you do deny it, you invite the battle to ensue.

"This is why you want to use this opportunity, and this moment, and acknowledge, 'I'm feeling doubt.' Let's do a Spontaneous Transformation session which I am going to teach you here. First stop and honor the belief that is coming up, even if you perceive it to be negative.

"How do you honor and acknowledge the fear? Just say, 'I'm really afraid.' Just feel it. Instead of saying, 'Oh, I'm not allowed to feel this way.' Can you feel the difference in that energy?"

Iris answers, "I think I can."

"Iris, that's going to stop your abundance right in their tracks," I point out, "Can you hear the doubt in your own 'yes?'"

Iris pauses to take in what I said, and returns by saying "Yes, now I can feel that."

"Yes, you are definitely on the right path because you are now holding the intention that everything is going to be fine.

"I remember when I was really, really broke, and I was two weeks away from living out of my car. I was driving and thinking, 'Okay, so am I okay, right now?' I realized that, in fact, in that particular moment, I was actually completely okay.

"'Okay, how about now?' I would ask myself, answering, 'Still good.' Even when we don't see a solution, we can still be okay in the moment, but we have to be in the moment.

"My doubt wanted to tell me something else, 'You don't have work. You don't have a job! You don't have a solution.' Then you just have to get back to the notion that you are okay in this moment."

I continue to ask Iris, "Can you see this for yourself?"

"Yes."

"So Iris, are you okay right now?" I query.

Smiling and getting it, Iris responds, "Yes, I'm okay right now."

The opportunity in doubt is the energy to check-in with yourself and see the okay-ness of yourself in the moment. Doubt wants to tell us that we're not going to be okay in the future because of something that happened in the past, but it denies the present moment.

Once you feel into your okay-ness in the moment, you've now established the vibrational resonance to now focus on creating the positive future you desire.

Asking Iris, "You still okay, right now?

Iris smiling more, "Yes, I am good right now."

I push on, "Can you feel the difference now between doubt and okay-ness? This is Spontaneous Transformation.

"So applying laws of attraction from this place of okay-ness, feel into what it would be like to find a job or an apartment that you really like. From this place of vibrational match, feel into the positive possibilities that exist in your future. Play with different ideas for yourself."

"Yes, that would be really nice," a relaxed, confident Iris answers.

"I call it the 'what if game'," as I remind Iris, "the 'what if game' gets played from the okay-ness space within yourself, and not the doubt place. By playing with it, it creates a feeling place, and an experience of abundance. Then, there is also the other side of this feeling of abundance when you are not in a good place and you are scared. Then you use that and feel scared. Allow yourself to feel fear and allow yourself to say, 'This feels like it's too much.' You don't have to be strong and brace yourself against it. You get to feel it."

Iris responds, "Yes. I have been working on that level as well, because if I try too hard to push these feelings away, it's overwhelming. I like the idea of practicing the 'what if game' in a playful manner and not analyzing it too much. Because the place I want to take it is, 'Well, this could never happen.'"

"The intent of the 'what if game' is to put your vibration at a frequency of possibility," I respond.

As Iris continued to work Spontaneous Transformation on doubt when it came up by shifting it to okay-ness and playing the 'what if game,' she was able to fine-tune deeper levels of inspiration. Inspiration is the well of which we want to create our reality and our futures. Action is taken when we are inspired. Inspired action has more impact than action for action sake. It's taking inspired action from a clear place of intention that creates the sequencing in the quantum field to design our hopeful future.

This means that you've cleared your thoughts, your worries, and your limited beliefs. When that space is created, it is unoccupied space. When we are so filled with worry, we can't hear what's next. In a moment, it might come back, and that's okay. But for the moment, you've cleared it, and you have this unoccupied space where you can hear the whispers of the Divine, and you can hear your soul sharing with you the path you should take.

When I was first inspired to reach out to Ellen Britt, who is now my coach, I was listening to her program and heard, "Send Ellen Britt an email and see if she wants to partner with you."

Now, I was no one, and she was someone with a big mailing list, but that's where the action comes in. I reached out to her, "I've got a product and I want to do a partnership with you." Ellen called me because she liked my product. She then decided, by talking to me, to start her own coaching program. From working with her, I learned the business model for Healing with the Masters. All of that came from hearing, "Send Ellen Britt an email." You act in that moment you are inspired. If I had listened to fearful thoughts like, "She doesn't know me from Adam, so why would she have anything to do with me?" I would have missed a huge opportunity.

Inspiration begins with listening. In order to do that, we need to create the space by creating that vibration of abundance by listening to ourselves and to what we want. We have to play with our energy so that we get to that place of unoccupied space, to listen to the Divine whispers, and then act on them as they happen. It's not about putting it on a list anywhere. It's about acting in the moment. But you can have a big, huge list. Most of the stuff on your list is not Divine inspiration. It's just stuff to do. The Divine inspiration comes in and says, "Do this now, now, now." And you trust in that moment.

The Fear that Motivates

Enough about the kind of fear that holds us back and stifles our love of life. Let's talk about the type of fear that we can embrace and use to push us forward. It can be pictured as a burning log, hot off the fire. This is the type of flame that we don't have to shy away from. Instead, we can view this fear as an indicator pointing us in the direction which our life wants to go. We can utilize this burning log as a torch, wielding it to illuminate the path we should dare to traverse. This type of fearful thinking is most often delivered in the framework of a phobia. For example, I have a fear of singing in public. I love to sing.

Singing is part of my practice. It's part of my gift, which I use to sing "soul songs" that come spontaneously from my heart. For some reason though, I have a fear of singing other artists' songs in front of an audience. There's no reason why I shouldn't, couldn't, or wouldn't want to expand beyond soul songs in the public realm, and that is why this fear is actually a blinking neon sign, pointing me in the direction of something that I am ready and prepared to explore.

As my experience shows, this type of fear is usually intermingled with goals or desires that are propelling you to the next step. These fears have to do with what you have a yearning to do, and a talent for, yet the trepidation prolongs your entering into the pursuit of those dreams. As you begin this journey of exploration, consider this: "Wouldn't it be nice if... when we journey down the path of exploration, our fears prove false and disappear as our deeper longings come true?"

Dissolving our debilitating fears may be a lifelong process because, as we grow, we continue to bring new challenges to us. However, you now have the tools to manage your own energy and approach to the energy of fear. You know it's just an energy that you can transform in partnership with your body's guidance. If you have done these practices, you have also cleared a wonderful space within where the fears once resided. You have begun creating a whole new vibrational blueprint to replace the old patterns that you don't need anymore because they don't serve your higher aspirations or your deeper truth. This next chapter takes that beautiful co-creation even further by re-patterning your experiences.

CREATING A NEW VIBRATIONAL BLUEPRINT

The Path to Wholeness Begins with Awareness

Through my years of healing and coaching work with clients, I have witnessed, over and over again, the power of looking inside to open the doors to positive change on every level. I have seen firsthand this technique of Spontaneous Transformation create real change in people's bodies, in their relationships, in their experience of abundance and in their enjoyment of life. Why does this work? Because when we look into the body, it allows us to see an internal aspect almost as an object that we can deal with and dismantle. Whether this object or aspect appears to you as a box, a cylinder, a feeling, a color or anything else, even as a sensation or emotion, it is in your presence and awareness to be treated with care, just as you would a loved one. It is there to serve you. In my visions, I have sensed my pain as something as small as a walnut. Yet, this little walnut contained within it a belief, a thought that built around it a hard shell to protect me.

If you can find that little part of yourself in your cellular memory, you can open it up and get the treasure of yourself back. Most of the time, whatever is there is protecting the self from emotional trauma so that the self can proceed in life.

The body is brilliant in its way of holding when needed
and releasing when you are ready.

The Observer Effect

This wonderful path to healing begins with simply observing that aspect of you, or listening to what it has been saying for years, and acknowledging it, "I hear you. I hear you. I see you." This is the miraculous aspect of the body that simulates the "Observer Effect" in quantum physics. My interpretation of this effect, in my own transformative work, is that simply observing an energy system as it expresses itself creates the space for that energy to shift. Most of the time, we do not want to look directly at our trauma because we think doing so will increase it and that's scary. The opposite is true – observing the residual emotional effects of painful memories created within the body can absolutely transform them when we allow it. We allow it when we are not invested in holding onto the pain which we let define us.

It is hard to revisit painful memories, and so it should be – we don't need to revisit them. In order to become who we truly are, we do need to acknowledge what is. See what has been left behind by trauma. Observing alone creates an opening. It is a place of disengagement that allows space for growth and discovery of greater aspects of ourselves.

When we raise our vibration, we open the space to hear the whispers of inspiration. We can see the signposts for what's next. When we are not being the observer of our experience, we just walk around feeling like the victim of our experience. It is as if we are walking down the street, pissed off, looking at the ground, fuming about "what happened to us." Then, as we walk around in our contracted energy, not present in the moment, we pass a huge, neon billboard to our right, flashing, "Turn left for your abundance!" and we don't see it. Then, at the next right is our true soul mate partner waving his or her arms, "I'm over here!" Up the street just ahead are thousands of customers waiting for us, but because we are distracted with upset, we miss all the signposts. We cannot feel the light feathers of inspiration tickling our senses, or the gifts waiting at every turn to nurture and prosper us, because we cannot feel anything other than the upset. As we open up the lines of communication within and come into greater resonance, all of those signs are still available to us along the path. When we resonate with what we want, synchronicities guide us so clearly to what we desire. We have eyes to see because we have "vibrational resonance" rather than dissonance.

Vibrational Resonance and Divine Discontent

We are by nature beings of joy, happiness and love - this is our basic essence. You might adamantly disagree at this stage and say, "I am not joy! If I were love and happiness, I wouldn't be reading this book." However, your soul knows this is true. Throughout our development, our natural state was co-opted, as our parents, peers, and hurtful circumstances appeared to "wound" us. I like to explain our natural progression by looking at ourselves as inverse butterflies. Meaning, we start as butterflies, or innocent beings of beauty and grace. As life progresses, we are wounded so we produce outer layers to protect ourselves that eventually form a tough, cocoon-like shell. Hurts, scars, psychic debris and negative beliefs from childhood and adolescence accumulate to impact our natural energy, until we are nesting and living within this cocoon made up of everything we are holding onto. From inside this cocoon, we view the world through a skewed vision. We are wary of the world so we throw up our defenses, even against the very things we want. We create the cyclical pattern of our life in which we continually live out the same emotional dynamics. The very walls we put up to protect us are the same ones that keep everything we want at bay.

When we ignore the patterns and dynamics, the volume increases. People and circumstances come along to nudge us and knock on the door, shouting at us to move inside and acknowledge what's showing up to be expressed. Some call it "the universal two-by-four." Things and people knock us over the head a few times to get our attention.

The good news is that our emotional scars, which form our protective barrier, do not change the truth of who we are. We are still those beings of grace and beauty that can fly whenever we want to. We all want to live a pain-free life. We all seek more peace, more joy, more happiness, and more abundance because we are seeking to go back to our natural state, to our authentic self. Fortunately, there is a path for every single one of us to get there.

The Compression Theory

After the awareness of something greater, the process initiates. The next phase of transformation begins when we ask for something different, a different energy and experience than what we have now. Yet, it doesn't necessarily come right away because if we are asking for something different, then we are focused on the fact that we are not experiencing it now. We are not yet in sync with what we want in that moment. If we were vibrating at the level of what we desired, we would already have what we are seeking and wouldn't have to ask. Instead, we start to come up against everything that represents what we don't want so that we can grow beyond it. I call it the compression theory.

When we decide what we want, we start thinking about all of our new dreams and desires. But, we haven't yet aligned our inner beliefs and experience with the higher vibration of those new energies we are seeking. It's still outside of us. So everything that is not what we want shows up.

> *Why would the opposite of what you want show up when it is not what you asked for? To be released, realigned and re-patterned so that you can make room for all those new energies! The greatest internal changes take place when we face life's biggest challenges.*

This creates a time of Divine discontent, during which we are hyper-aware of everything we don't want. This is when we are nudged and guided to seek answers, to take a new direction, to face the truth of ourselves and to change old ways of doing things. The journey to your truth begins when you ask for it. The catch – and the gift – is that we now have to deliberately raise our vibration level. It is up to us to seek a new vibration level that matches what we asked for.

When I say, "you asked for it," I mean your soul asks for it, and seeks its own growth. Sometimes that growth doesn't come easily or in the way we expect. There is an old saying that the Divine does not give us more than we can handle. Well, I go one step further to say, "The Divine gives us the growth opportunities we want and are ready for." In Dr. Bernie Siegel's best-selling book, *Peace, Love, and Healing,* the doctor takes a holistic approach with his cancer patients describes this phenomenon by saying, "Facing death is often the catalyst that enables people to reach out for what they want."

When we are ready for change, the universe gives us the lessons we need in order to get what we want. When we face the most difficult challenges, we begin to live for what truly matters. When we face illness, loss, a traumatic event, or re-live an unhealthy relationship cycle again and again, the universe is turning up the volume knob, so that we will listen to the call to live a deeper life. It is as if we are driving down the road of life, and we pass a sign that reads: "Dear Driver, There is a Deeper, More Meaningful Way to Live and You are Missing It!" Many of us ponder this for a moment, then stomp on the gas pedal, and career on down the same road in the same direction we were already traveling. When we hit roadblocks and challenges over and over again, we are finally forced to listen to the call to change and pursue the truth of what we came here to do.

Change doesn't have to be this difficult. But if we continue to deny the soul's desire to grow, it will do what it can to turn us around and get us on the easier road. Humans are beings of energy. When we tune-in to our core energy, we feel love, joy and abundance. Our core energy operates on a high vibrational level. This is what I refer to as "flow" because this is when our energy is flowing in a healthy manner. This natural state is the foundational opportunity for abundance, for love, for balance, creation and health. Each of these qualities is the essence of who we are. What is interesting and unexpected about our experience is this:

Our experiences reflect back to us exactly where we are in our process that matches our vibrational resonance.

Family Issues: A Story

Here is a good example of the compression theory in action.

Dave called into *MasterWorks Healing Membership Site* with a family issue. His older brother had just died. This tragic experience led Dave to seek a more loving experience with his family. So Dave took it upon himself to organize a family vacation. His family was dispersed throughout the country and had been distant for a while. His mother had often complained that the family would not be in the same room again until her funeral. He decided to reunite the family in order to honor his mother. Dave was also hoping that this would provide a space for his own healing – he had always felt like his mother had treated him as the "second best" son in the family. Growing up, his perception of his experience told him that his mother had shown preferential attention to her other children. In essence, he was seeking a new vibration level in the form of more love, acceptance and family unity. But his vision didn't turn out the way he'd planned.

According to Dave, during the week that his family came together over his brother's death, an unexplainable rift seemed to happen between him and his family. The rest of his family did not seem to share his honorable intention to reunite his family so that they could bond and express more love. As Dave sought a higher emotional vibration that would feel better, all of the conflicting vibrations and emotional states rose to the surface to be revealed. His intention (higher vibrating energy) and the family's (lower vibrating energies) were not in resonance with each other and could not be contained in the same space. These vibrational differences created an opportunity for either a change or a rift to occur. Unfortunately, for their family, it created a rift. Dave was motivated by Divine discontent: the point at which your life becomes so uncomfortable, that you finally become aware that something vital within yourself needs to change in order to force a positive change in your experience. What he encountered was the Compression Theory: that once you set that high-resonating intention to change, the universe gives you exactly the opportunity you need to *be* that.

The growth comes from challenging situations which help you develop that quality.

Dave's desire was to love and be loved. He could feel it, see it and sense it, yet, he wasn't in vibrational resonance with it, so it didn't happen the way he wanted. The experience still served him, as painful as it was. Everything showed up that needed to be resolved. He got to experience this next level of awareness, and began to put his new intentions into practice after working through some remaining emotional dissonance. His mother never changed, but he no longer held an expectation of her which gave Dave peace.

Searching Outside Ourselves

For many of us, when we experience times of compression or challenge, we become stuck because we are looking outside ourselves for a solution. When we look outside ourselves, we try tactics, or try to change others, or perhaps we reach for alcohol, drugs, sex, relationships, or food to fulfill us. When we're looking outside of ourselves for someone to blame, these are moments of being out of "flow." To move toward change, and a healthy energy flow, requires us to go within to connect with our heart and allow whatever shows up to guide us.

It is clear from the challenges within our world – the economy, the environment, the divorce rate, etc. – that something has to change. Actually, it is our way of *being* in the world that needs to change. The change we seek doesn't have to come through sacrifice and suffering, and the path to peace will not come by pointing fingers in blame.

Searching Inside Ourselves

While I don't personally believe any of us are ever truly stuck, the wonderful thing about the perception of stuckness is that it provides us the opportunity to reach within ourselves to pursue our joy, our love, and to know acceptance. Why do we think we are stuck? Well, again, it goes back to the notion that challenges arrive because we are ready for the change it will bring. Life is compressing us. We are asking for something that's really big or, at least, bigger than what we have. We want to be healthier, or wealthier, or happier. Or maybe we want to finally be in a loving relationship.

The opening to all of that begins with our saying, "I am allowed to want. I deserve happiness. I want what I desire and that is a better, easier experience." In truth, all that the universe wants for us is the same good that we desire – our fullest joy and expression of love and a fulfilling life. As we journey toward an awakening of our authentic selves, we begin to enlarge the way we dream. We don't want to just get by or just pay off the mortgage. We want financial freedom, a healthier loving connection with others, a deeper significance and satisfaction in what we do, or a greater impact on the world. We're allowed to have all that! So why do we not have that big life... yet? It is usually because our old beliefs, old ways of being, old patterns of behavior embedded within us are not in resonance with this bigger life. We are still holding onto something that is holding us back.

Every time we are not experiencing what we want,
it is an opportunity for us to clear and release trauma and
become in vibrational resonance with that which we want.

When we are searching for answers, or for a better experience, the universe (which is really us) will always heed our call and show us what is not in vibrational resonance with our desires and, therefore, needs to be released. That is when we can see our challenges for what they are. They are no longer the same patterned challenges that have haunted us forever... now they are wonderful opportunities for us to stop, to notice, to pay attention, and to look inside! To change what is on the inside will change your experience outside.

Changing Your Vibrational Blueprint

Did you notice in the previous chapters' Spontaneous Transformation sessions that, as the participant told their "story" of what happened to them, I assisted them in experiencing a brand new story of possibility? Offering new interpretations created positive alternatives and choices around how they saw an old, repetitive issue and how they could now view themselves. This is another aspect of the Spontaneous Transformation called re-patterning. It is an important step that layers in new experiences and changes the participant's vibrational blueprint.

The body cannot tell the difference between the story we tell that "happened to us" and the new story we create. The story represents the new vibrational reprint. In that still point of listening and loving the self, we see our story and ourselves in a brand new way. Instead of "dad always yelling made mom leave," for example, the participant creates a completely different story from a larger vantage point. Shifting perception shifts family dynamics in that it allows for new possibilities to present themselves. The result is a new energetic for the self; therefore, everyone else involved. The story creates a new foundation and template from which to live.

Re-patterning can also be used to let go of energies that are not our own. Sometimes things show up in our bodies that actually belong to someone else and got imprinted in our vibrational blueprint. Examples would be a mother's critical voice, a father's consistent anger or family grief. These things are learned behaviors and imprinted energies that we carry, but in fact don't belong to us. We take them on for survival, as they constitute the rules of the world we entered into. The pattern allows us to energetically "fit in."

This is when the true purpose of Spontaneous Transformation comes into play: to clear and cleanse lower vibrations in the body, subsequently making us available to all the good we desire.

When we raise our vibrations, we resonate with the flow
of universal joy and love and peace and happiness and harmony.
We experience ourselves as we are.

The following simple technique allows the body to experience what it is to disengage from this "other" part of the self, voice or emotional energy. The disengagement creates space for who you really are to be revealed.

Re-patterning Your Experience: Practice

Here is a simple four-step process to practice on a regular basis to clear your energy field and reclaim your truer essence, energy, and thereby your experience:

1) Use the Spontaneous Transformation to move into the body and access the part of you which you suspect is not you. Ask it: *Are you part of me?*

The part you want to understand better could be a tone of voice or an unwanted state such as a level of anger, a constant fear or chronic sadness. Think about whatever is showing up that doesn't seem to be an integral part of you. It might be you, but there's a good chance that it's not and that it's just learned behavior.

How do you know it's not you? When you ask: "Are you a part of me?" you hear it, but you don't experience it as you. Maybe you experience it as if it's something you're watching. Perhaps you sense that it has you, but you don't have it.

Once you understand what it is, now you have *it*. It no longer has *you*. You can now choose to move it.

2) Ask: *Would it be okay if you move just outside of my energy field?*

Work in partnership with that aspect, gently request it move outside of your energy field just for a moment. You can even hold the intention that it could come back if, perhaps, it serves you. This creates a space of allowing; and it will move outside of your energy field.

3) Experience your body as it stays outside of you.

Stay fully in your body and notice: "What does your body feel like without that energy signature?" It's usually calm, peace, loving, and in alignment. What is there in its place is a truer experience of who you are. Take a good look at this because this is who you are. Feel into it. Enjoy it and, prolong this new energy so it becomes more familiar and comfortable without that "other" aspect.

4) Ask the aspect outside of your field: *What needs to happen now?*

Now that the anger or critical voice is outside of you, and you are still standing and presumably feeling good, realize that this could be your new vibrational blueprint if you choose it. By asking it what needs to happen now, aspects of that energy might reintegrate because they were powerful supporters or teachers for you. What happens in most cases is that you may see or feel that aspect melt away, or appear to be taken away by a crane, or silence may simply replace it. Guides may even come in to release the energy permanently from your field. You will be left with new, clean energy.

This may not be the last time you will have to do this, by the way, depending on how entrenched that aspect was within your self-identity. The process of becoming ourselves is never completed. We came here to explore this beautiful universe where spirit indwells. This might be just one aspect of the beautiful pattern that is you right now; it will lift in time when it is ready. When we get into a partnership role with our body, we play with these aspects and have more freedom to choose them or not. When we take an adversarial role with ourselves, our response when those aspects return is often like, "I did this twenty years ago! I'm still dealing with this? What's wrong with me?" When we recognize it as a chance for us to be more loving with ourselves, we can come into a playful relationship with what is. We can allow those "alien" aspects of the self to guide us to a deeper and more expansive experience of who we really are.

CHAPTER

Five

THE BODY JOURNEY

The body and brain connection is an amazing thing. The best part of it is that it is not hard-wired, meaning we truly can rewire those visceral connections and shift the way we experience the past through how we think about it!

This chapter is all about reclaiming your body's experience by shifting how you hold trauma in the mind and memory. For example, memory associated with trauma is in a part of the brain that is connected to the sympathetic nervous system, which creates fight or flight responses from fear, whether real or imagined. It creates and recreates a visceral, full-body response every time you stimulate that memory. You stimulate the memory every time you tell and retell that story as if you are making the body relive it on some level. Once you re-pattern the memory, however, its associative pattern moves to another area in the brain where it is detached emotionally. It becomes just like any other memory. You may still have access to it, but it no longer causes you to re-experience it.

The Consistency Theory

It is especially useful to know this place inside when we are in the presence of old feelings associated with particular people who serve as triggers. My consistency theory says that: people are nothing if not consistent in their behavior. So, at some point, to take care of ourselves, it becomes our own responsibility to respond differently to other people's consistent reactions. For example, your mother or father may respond in a predictable way every time certain issues arise... they are consistent. You may recognize a pattern in your partner in which they get angry, then remorseful, then loving, then angry again.

Believe it or not, there is an alternative to reacting in your own consistent way to their predictably consistent behavior. You can stop before going down that same road or engaging in that same conversation which always has the same outcome, and instead do an internal examination and dialoguing to see what is triggered, creating new responses from a new place of understanding and love for yourself.

In light of what we know about someone else's consistent behavior, we can change the otherwise predictable dynamic by choosing a new response. We can maintain our loving relationship while, at the same time, protecting ourselves from repeatedly stimulating the same old trauma.

Read through the whole chapter before you try these practices. When you are observing a traumatic event from your past, the key is to not return to the original trauma in a way that allows the same feelings of the past to flood your body again now. It's unnecessary. For release to take place, simply observe and acknowledge the memory and the emotions that were brought forth at that time, so you can bring new light to your understanding of what's happening. This is an important part of letting go of the tension and pain that resulted from a traumatic incident or repetitively hurtful situation. In other words, maintain the larger perspective of having already made it through to the present to a safe place within.

The point here is to understand what you made that memory *mean* in your mind so that you can process it and get beyond it. You are an interested observer of the past here, *not* a participant. This next one is for the purpose of releasing the body's holding of trauma, past or current.

Release Trauma Without Re-experiencing It: Practice

1) *Move to a safe place within your center.*

Find a comfortable place, either lying or sitting with your back supported. Take several deep breaths with the intention to oxygenate your body and relax. The breath starts just below the belly button, which is the first to rise. (You can put your hand there to check.) The chest rises next and the shoulders rise last, but only slightly. Breathing need not be forced. Imagine the last moment of the inward breath filling the very uppermost part of your lungs. At the top of that breath, it should feel as if you are giving your shoulders and neck an internal massage.

From this point of relaxation, go inside your body and find the place that feels like it is your center. Drift down into your body, like a pearl sinking slowly and gently down through water. When the pearl stops, that is your center. Find a still point in this center. The resting point of the pearl is the still point, the pearl's home, and your sacred chamber. It's slightly below and behind the heart. If thoughts are floating around in your head, as in water, wait for them to sink to the bottom so that your mind is clear.

Now picture the pearl outside the body, floating above your head. I want you to notice that pearl is you! That's the purest essence of you. People often observe the pearl's layers of energy either humming or shedding light. Allow that glowing pearl to gently drop down into your head, reminding you who you are throughout every cell. As it moves past the thymus gland, it's emanating life force ripples outward, expanding into the extremities of the body, down the arms and ripples back up to the center and back out. Within every center of every cell, it reminds you who you are. All the layers of love.

Bringing it home, back to the center, feel all the love and peace as you notice something – your connection to the Divine. That Divine witnesses you witnessing it. It returns the wave of love, knowing you, loving you, adoring you.

If thoughts wander through again, fold them as if they were pieces of cloth and lay them aside. Feel exceptionally loved and supported before turning your attention into the body. This is your platform of knowing from which to ask body to reveal places where trauma is held. There may be places of pain calling out to you, "Over here! I really want to talk to you!" Remember who you really are as you visit those places.

2) *Observe the body's holding of the traumatic experience.*

From this place of safety, bring your attention to the place in your body. Pretend your eyes are inside your body and you can see this place of tension or pain. This is the most important piece of this technique – go to it and observe it without judgment or assessment. Just see: *What does it look like?* Some see an object or color (glass, cylinder, box, house, toy, black hole, red, etc.), some have a feeling sense (soft, hard, gooey, sharp, heavy, etc.), and some sense it as an emotion (anger, vulnerability, confusion, etc.).

3) *Dialogue with what is present while allowing it to change.*

Having brought your complete attention to this place inside your body, take a close look and start your internal dialogue. Describe, in detail, to yourself what you are seeing and feeling in that place of tension or pain. Notice if it changes and observe the change. Remember the Observer Effect: your body is happy to see you here and wants to show you something. It will use a language of symbols that you will understand to communicate its needs. That alone can change the whole dynamic. Watch the changes as you have the following conversation with this aspect of your body.

Ask into it and wait for clear answers. They can arise as a feeling, a sentence or a picture:

- Why are you (the thing you are observing) here?
- What is this about?
- Do you have something in particular to show me?
- Notice if it changes. If it does, ask: Why did you change?
- How has having this (shape, feeling, sound, and sense) served me?
- Where do you come from? When did you originate? Was it a specific event? A time in your life? An uncomfortable conversation? A physical injury? Some abusive incident? An accident? And so on.
- Am I willing to release this? If so, how can I resolve or release this? You are not looking for an answer or command here, such as: "go exercise more," or "lose weight." Be patient for the answer you know is right and true. You will recognize when it is coming from your source.
- What does releasing this "thing" look or feel like in your body in this moment?

4) *Observe the changes as it releases.*

The observed area will shift and change to find a pattern of balance. It may even release completely in this form. When the shift occurs, it might feel like a big sigh, tears may come, or laughing. Heat is often released and sometimes there is a pulsing energy or vibration. Gurgling in the colon is also evidence of shifting energies. These are all forms of energetic release.

5) *If another area of the body calls for your attention, repeat steps 2-4.*

As it shifts and releases, notice the rest of your body. Is there tension somewhere else? The experience of release can be like peeling an onion: one release opens the opportunity for a new area that was likely related to that area which was holding. If that first area seems to be connected to another part of the body, go to that new place that is calling you and do the exercise again. Use this technique daily, or even several times a day, if it feels right.

6) *Acknowledge the changes that you observed.*

I recommend finishing this exercise using the Ho'oponopono prayer. It assists you to thank the body, be grateful for the learning, and love yourself for creating this opportunity for true change to occur in your life.

Here is the Ho'oponopono prayer in its entirety:

"I'm sorry. Please forgive me. I love you. Thank you."

Re-Writing Our Stories to Change Our Vibrational Blueprint

We all have stories. Some sad stories start out like a bad country song: someone (your parents, friends, boss, partner…) has "done you wrong." We dwell on those stories of negative incidents because they are still held in our bodies. Often, they are still held in our bodies because we continue to dwell on the past in a way that keeps it in place. Otherwise, we would have no reason to repeat the incident over and over in our mind or our experience. Our bodies are perfect diagnostic tools for our emotional and unconscious states of habitual dysfunction. When we choose to hold onto an old, negative story in our bodies, with all its lower-vibrating emotional content, it acts like a big rock in the river of our lives, slowing down our energy current. When our natural energy is not flowing as well as it could, we can get sick and feel physical pain or negative (lower-vibrating) emotions and mental fatigue (memory loss, etc.). It also means, with all that old debris still floating around unresolved, we can't take the straight path to what we want. It holds back all the good that would otherwise flow to us.

The opportunity is to get clear of our stories. Once we see how the drama has played out internally as our beliefs, and externally as the events in our lives, we have the best opportunity to re-write our story the way we want it to be.

If you recall from Chapter 4, Dave had organized a family reunion after his older brother died. His hopes were for that gathering to provide a space for healing the past and strengthening the familial bonds, especially with his mother. He still felt as he did growing up, that his mother consistently showed preferential treatment toward her other children while treating Dave with distant reserve. In fact, at the end of this family vacation, she hugged her other son goodbye then got in her car without saying goodbye to Dave. Dave walked over to the car and knocked on the window. His mother simply rolled down the window and said, "Thanks for the nice week."

Dave was extremely hurt when he called in to the *MasterWorks Healing Membership Site* to work around this issue. Spontaneous Transformation allowed me to coach Dave into "writing a new story."

Feeling Unloved and Unappreciated: A Spontaneous Transformation

From a cognitive perspective, there are a couple of things going on for Dave. Dave had a lovely vision and created an opportunity for his family to come together. This triggered everyone's pattern, including his mother's: her consistent lack of affection and lack of sharing love with him. So, by just recognizing that, we get to understand what happened.

I used to say, "I'm shocked and I'm shocked that I'm shocked." Because, when others responded in a certain way and I got upset and triggered, I had to realize that that occurrence happened that same way since I was born, so why would I be upset now? And it's likely because there's a part of us that hasn't resolved it.

What I'd like to do with Dave in this process is to get to that piece of him that hasn't resolved this. First, we need to understand the cognitive piece of all of this so that we understand that when we're hurt, it's ours. I have this other saying, which is, "When it sticks to you, it's yours." I've gotten to a point where certain things that consistently caused me upset don't stick anymore. I can pretty much predict to a 99.9 percentile how certain and familiar people are going to respond to specific situations.

Most of us can relate to this with the familiars of our family, friends, and co-workers. The next time we put ourselves in that situation, and we have a reaction to it, it's like, "Well, there's a part of me now that needs to be responsible for the fact that they're going to act exactly the same way, and I can choose to be hurt or not."

How do we choose to not be hurt? First of all, by acknowledging it, noticing it, and paying attention to it. The second piece is to actually go inside and do your work around it. I like to do the tapping of the heart. I ask my client's to bring their energy into their body. Just tap your heart – thump, thump, thump, and thump. As you feel that tapping, feel as if you have a nose in your heart and, as you breathe with that nose, it brings your attention into that area. As you feel your attention in your heart, I want you to bring your attention also into that sacred chamber – into that place in the center of your body, in the center of your being.

Now, I ask Dave during our session to enter that beautiful sacred place, "Do you have access to that place in your heart?"

Dave affirmatively responds.

As I continue talking him through the process, I say, "Good. I want you to feel that atmosphere of your heart. Shift that movement into a new place, a new energy, a place of connection, and a place of support. Good. As you feel that support there, know that this is where your deepest connection to yourself, to your being, is. This is you connected to you. This is also you connected to the Divine, to the Divine energy. Then this is where your true love comes from. This is where the goddess of love and the god of love, the feminine and the masculine, meet to deliver love in its purest form to you.

"The relationships we have on the earth plane are simply reminding us of this energy. There we go, right now. Do you feel that energy of love?"

A relaxed Dave affirmatively responds.

I continue saying, "It's all for you, just for you. As you feel that energy, you feel the energy of love. You actually amplify the energy of love, so that it opens up even more. As it opens up even more, you can feel that vibrational blueprint of remembering, 'Oh, yes.' I think one of the things you came down to work with on this planet is love. You're a loving man.

"And you've had people in your life that didn't reflect that love back to you quite so much so that you could, in turn, understand love more. Does that make sense?"

Dave follows along.

I continue, "That's in part what your mom is, that reflection. We're going to do a little re-patterning right now. Re-patterning is creating a new story around your mom. This will be a new story which allows the body to feel a new vibrational blueprint that you can use instead of that old feeling and that old trigger with that person – even as they go about doing exactly what they've always done. Now we won't be reacting to it."

In the 1980s, Dennis Waitley, a founding member of the National Council for Self-Esteem, worked with the Olympic team. He was one of the first to do visualization and test it. They had these athletes all hooked up to brainwave monitors. What they discovered was the body could not tell the difference between the race that was run in their head through visualization, and the race that was run on the track. We can apply this to the stories of the people in our lives as well.

"We create a new vibrational resonance. What we're going to do right now is a re-patterning with your mom, Dave. Feel into that sacred chamber again. Feel the essence of support and love that's still and always there for you. Now, from this beautiful sacred chamber of support and love, I want you to feel when you really noticed these differences between you and your siblings, and that you sensed you were second choice. How old were you when you got that?"

"I was probably about eight years old at the time," answers Dave.

I say, "I want you to bring your attention to that little eight-year-old. I want you to sense the beautiful, gorgeous, loving and honorable adult that you are right now. Bring that adult attention to the child that is you. Now you are just there for him, supporting him. He knows that you're present. He feels your presence. He can sense your presence. As he's feeling that presence, I want you to feel how he feels when he recognizes, 'wow, this is how it feels like to be heard, to be really heard.' What does that feel like, Dave, for him, for that eight-year-old?"

Dave answers, "Joy."

I continue, "Yes, he's really appreciative. He just didn't know what that felt like. Now, there's this wonderful man, all grown up. Your little one is looking at you. The little one that is you is looking at you saying, 'Wow! Look at me. I'm pretty cool. I grew up. I made it! I made it through this. I'm doing okay.' How does that feel? Can you see the wonder in his eyes?"

Dave nods affirmatively.

I continue, "Good. If you're feeling a little emotion come up in that moment, allow it. If there are tears, let them come up.

"Now we're going to do a little exercise. The boy's feeling hurt, and he's telling you a few things. He's sharing, 'Oh my gosh, this happened and this happened.' You may not hear the actual words of the story. The story does not matter. What I want you to feel is the essence of him sharing and being heard. That's what this is about. That's what all of communication is about ultimately. It isn't the words in the story. It's the essence of being heard and acknowledged.

"So he's just telling you a few things that happened and that he was really confused and you're just responding, 'Oh yes, okay. I hear you. Oh, that one hurt.' You might look into his eyes, and say something like, 'I'm so sorry that happened to you. I'm so sorry. I'm here.'

"Next we're going to work with your mother. Right now, we've got this little cloak of invisibility over your little guy. So he's going to go right up to your mom and get to a place where he can see her really clearly. Now, she can't see him, but he can see her.

"As you're looking at her, I want you to watch, just watch. You've got this adult perspective that you're back here as this eight-year-old watching your mom and the adult that is you is looking, too. I want you to see the tension that she holds in different places in her body. Can you see that?"

Dave answers "Yes."

"I want you to see that there is – oh, I," I pause to feel into what I'm about to say, "I can feel a grinding of the teeth. You know when you see someone clenching, is that true?"

Dave answers again, "Yes."

"And there's wringing of the hands," as I grab the visualization in my own mind, I continue saying, "It's like that energy, but with the composure that's hiding the wringing of the hands. Is that true?"

Dave, "Uh-huh."

"As you're watching her, I want you to also notice something really interesting. She also has a sacred chamber. As you look at her sacred chamber, you can see that, wow," I say excitedly, "she's got a place inside of her that's connected to the Divine energy. She's got a place inside of her that is pure love. Wow, look at that! What does your mom's sacred chamber look like, Dave?"

Dave responds, "I'm not sure."

I say, "It's hard to see hers. Your little guy really knows it's there, and he's kind of amazed. He didn't realize that it was in there. As you look at your mom's sacred chamber, I want you to notice now that there's also a lot of muck and guck around there, isn't there?"

Dave knowingly says, "Yes, there is."

Not wanting to be critical of Dave's mother, I explain the mechanism of belief, thought, and trauma. "What happens is that the trauma gets stuck in the body and what you're looking at in the muck and the guck is her life traumas that got held in her body."

What happens is that every intention of every single human on the planet starts from the sacred chamber, from a place of love, of pure love and pure intent. As intention gets filtered out of the sacred chamber through the muck and guck of trauma and the beliefs that the trauma set up, it shows up in the world as something other than what was intended. This impacts how we view others in the world which was what was happening with Dave's mother.

I continue on with Dave by saying, "Your little boy is kind of amazed at this, too. He's got kind of a mechanical mind, that little guy, doesn't he? He's amazed at the mechanics of intention. As he's looking at his mom, he realizes that a lot of the things that she is reacting to, when it comes to little Dave, have nothing to do with him. That she is in reaction to what the trauma (a.k.a. muck and guck) is triggering in her.

"There is a nice shift there. I'm just kind of holding the energy of that shift which that little guy is getting, 'Wow, this really wasn't about me. This is just all she was dealing with.'

"Something really amazing is happening right now as your little boy is realizing this. The person you're looking at, your mom, Dave, has the chance now for the first time to really see her own sacred chamber, her light. This is what happens with the observer effect: when we observe someone else in wholeness, they have the chance to experience that wholeness as well. And now, she's noticing it. She's seeing it. She's experiencing it. She's feeling it. And she is going, 'Wow, I have this inside of me.' Is this true? Is this real for you Dave?"

Dave responds, "My body is just getting really hot."

"Yes," I affirm, "There is a lot of emotional release happening here."

"On the inside, it's in the lower abdomen area," Dave describes.

"Is it comfortable that it's getting hot?" I ask checking in with Dave.

He assures me that he is okay, and we continue on with the process.

"Now you are watching your mom discover her sacred chamber, her place of connection with the Divine energy within. This is the way that vibration works. As she notices it, she can't help but vibrate at a higher state. Even a little bit higher, breaks up the density. I believe there is a softening occurring within her," I say as I notice.

Dave agrees.

"Now, remember Dave, we're doing a re-patterning here so we're creating a new story," I say as I remind Dave the intent here of this part of the Spontaneous Transformation.

He says, "Yes."

"The new story goes like this – as your mother begins to soften, things shift, she drops density, and she starts to notice that little boy. There is a safety within him knowing that his mother is shifting, moving into a place of alignment with that loving sacred chamber energy.

"What happens is, as your mom does that, there's clarity of vision within her now, too. She looks over at her little boy and can see him now. She sees him in a new way. She sees him in a way that has less density of reaction. She sees him in a way that is, 'Oh my god, this is a beautiful little boy. This is my son, my second born.' Can you take this new story into your being with your little eight-year-old self?"

Dave replies, "Yes."

"As you feel this new re-patterned moment, this new blueprint we're creating of connection, of love that your mother actually does have for you..." I say this from my own deepest knowing, "I want you to know that this is real because, as you saw, every one of us has this sacred chamber within us that has the purest intentions of love always. Sometimes we lose touch with that and sometimes our loved ones lose it. As she's hugging you in this moment, you know that this is real. There's a piece of your mom that has shifted and can hug you now. It may not be an obvious thing that you see in three-dimensional reality right now with her, but there's a shift and this vibrational shift can't help but shift all. How does that feel, Dave?"

Dave explains, "It feels good. A warmth seems to have dissipated. I've got more of a bright light within than I did."

Now in the process, I focus the attention to Dave as himself today, and say, "Bring your energy back in and feel that sacred chamber. Does it feel different, Dave?"

"Yes, Jennifer," he responds, "In the beginning it was dark, like a dark red and now it's like a light blue much cooler."

The opportunity for re-patterning in Spontaneous Transformation is to go back and listen to this experience again and again, several times, because we're setting up a new vibrational blueprint. We're setting up a space and an energy for people to go there again and build that memory muscle, build that vibrational blueprint until it's really a part of your energy system, your mind, and your heart.

Dave's therapeutic experience exemplifies the process of "re-writing our story" to replace our negative experience with a positive vibrational blueprint. Just as Dave did, you can re-write those painful stories of rejection, hurt, victimhood, etc. Through re-writing our stories, we create a pattern of experiencing the emotions that we want to feel, recreating our life experience from then forward. We may not have had a choice initially in terms of the trauma we've suffered; however, we do have the choice whether to let our negative stories continue to victimize us OR to retell them the way we experience life. In this way, we see ourselves and others in a new light.

If Dave's experience has inspired you, walk through the steps of re-writing your own story. When you talk about your old stories, and are still victimized by them in your mind, you are reinforcing the energy which attracts more of the same. Use this exercise to move you into what you really want. This creates a permanent momentum which rushes forward to meet you where you are; allowing yourself to go to the place you truly want to be, not just what your mind tells you is possible. Match your vibrational resonance with the story you want instead. Use your body as the anchor for those positive feelings.

Re-Writing Your Story: Practice

1) Tell yourself your own negative story of victimhood, how someone did you wrong, and give it plenty of emotion, but don't re-experience it. Just tell it as if you are reporting just how bad it was. Stay neutral about the story.

2) Using the internal body observational techniques you learned above, what does that story feel like in your body? Feel it, see it and/or hear it. Where in your body are you feeling this negative emotion?

3) Now, say to yourself out loud, "I don't want to feel this anymore. I am ready to experience something new."

4) Next, ask yourself, "What do I WANT to feel?" Connect and anchor into your solar plexus and heart area to help identify what it is you want to feel instead.

5) Move this new, positive feeling sense from your mind (where most of us think we are feeling) into your body.

What does it feel like in your body to have the new positive energies that you want? What does it feel like in your body to feel peace? To feel joy? To feel confidence? To feel abundance? Where in your body do you feel these glorious energies? Stay in your body and really feel these new, positive energies take root.

6) Take it to the next level now – describe what your life looks like with these feelings. Tell this new story with as much emotional investment in it as you used to have for the past story you held. Use the anchored feeling you discovered in your body to affix it into the visualization of your life and the ways in which it appears when you are really congruent with these positive energies. How does your body feel now in these new energies? What experiences come naturally now that you feel so different from the past? What now flows to you that is aligned with this new vibrational blueprint?

7) Take that story of what you want back into your body again and feel it. Imagine that you are storing it there and that you can access it anytime. It will be there for you. The body remembers. Give it as long as it takes to adjust to how wonderful it now feels to be you.

Now that you know how to get to those deep places inside where trauma is stored, and what you want to replace them with, it's time to clear and cleanse what is held there.

Six

CLEARING and CLEANSING

Can you recall a time a loved one or friend hurt you? I mean really hurt you to the point where you just couldn't let go of it? Do you recall how long you held angry feelings and thoughts towards that person? If we are honest, every one of us has harbored bitter or resentful feelings toward someone whom we believe hurt us. What we don't often realize is how powerful these thoughts are. Our thoughts, in fact, are not confined to the walls of our mind; instead, like the seeds of dandelions blown into the wind, they move outward throughout our body and into the world and take root. Similarly, our thoughts travel into the universe as a creative force and give birth to reality.

Clearing and cleansing our storehouse of resentments provides us the opportunity to realign our thoughts with what lies even deeper within our hearts and, ultimately, changes our reality. Here are some very specific routes you can take to discover those wonderful places within beyond all suffering.

Resolving the Past: The Ho'oponopono Way

We could all use a major housecleaning from time to time to reassess what we are carrying from the past and hindering our experience of flow. This practice uses the intention of the ancient Hawaiian prayer of Ho'oponopono, which is ultimately self-forgiveness. Added to it is a layer of Spontaneous Transformation, which brings the experience of forgiveness into the body and, therefore, into the present and out of the past. So it is a hybrid of my own creation that begins with the recognition that we have felt hurt, and an acknowledgment that we have also hurt others. However unintentional or intentional it was, it was the only way we knew to cope.

The ability to forgive others is rooted in recognizing the humanity of those who have wounded us, then looking in the mirror and honestly acknowledging our own reflection.

Perhaps the reflection of our humanity does not take on the same form or behaviors of the person who hurt us, but has a reflective component within us somewhere. At this point, some of us may object, "But I never cheated on my husband and he did that to me," or "I never betrayed my friend the way she betrayed me." Even if you haven't hurt someone else in the extreme way they hurt you, you have betrayed a person in some way, however small, in your words, deeds, or thoughts. Remember our thoughts, although seemingly innocuous, are incredibly creative and powerful. In fact, they create our reality in every moment. So when we have a really bad thought about someone, that's a creative force in the universe.

At the same time, our positive thoughts act as an even more powerfully creative force. In fact, a positive thought is a thousand times more powerful than a negative thought. We can overcome our negative thoughts through clearing and cleansing, realigning and re-patterning. In order to go through this process, we might want to recognize the places within us that need forgiveness, even if our transgressions were only in our mind.

We develop behavioral responses – like anger, lashing out, jealousy, controlling, and victim mentality – which act as coping mechanisms to protect ourselves. However, the adaptive way which we behave that formed around an old wound can end up hurting someone else. So we recognize that we are all in a learning process. When we begin to acknowledge how others have hurt us because of their own coping mechanism, and how we have expressed an analogous coping mechanism back into the world, we gain an understanding that provides the foundation for forgiveness – of the self and others. In other words, compassion.

The Ho'oponopono Prayer as Spontaneous Transformation

Here is the Ho'oponopono prayer in its entirety:
"I'm sorry. Please forgive me. I love you. Thank you."

I'M SORRY.

The purpose of saying "I'm sorry" is self-forgiveness. "I'm sorry" addresses the times that we have blamed ourselves for the trauma we've experienced. The expression of an apology expresses empathy and acknowledgment that somebody felt hurt. And that someone is you. It's not, "I'm sorry that I did this." It's: "I'm sorry that this thing happened to me and that I created a coping mechanism that may have hurt someone else." We recognize and honor the wounds we've experienced, the blame we've internalized, and the various ways we learned to protect ourselves and survive.

PLEASE FORGIVE ME.

This second line recognizes times that we have hurt, angered, damaged, or disrespected someone else with this coping mechanism. We forgive ourselves, knowing we did the best we could. We are also asking the Divine for forgiveness and can feel it is an automatic given. It is humbling, which is healing.

I LOVE YOU.

We have the choice to be loving with ourselves or not. This is where we recognize the Divine within and appreciate who we are with the deep love and compassion which we would give a child or loved one. In turn, as we experience this in our recognition of ourselves, we can see the Divine even within those who have hurt, abused or damaged us. Some people have challenges with this step. Self-love is so healing, it is worth your life to ask into the body what is holding you back from a full experience of it. Sometimes, actively loving the self over and over through this prayer becomes its own cleansing of the soul.

THANK YOU.

Lastly, we say "thank you" to the person in our lives who showed up to teach us this lesson; they showed up because we were ready to release an aspect of the pattern. We thank ourselves for going through this process. We are also thanking the universe for showing us what we need to clear and cleanse. We express our gratitude for help in the releasing process.

Finding Peace Through Forgiveness: Practice

Let's get started. Go ahead and dig into whoever has been challenging you so that you can feel a complete emotional and physical release from the situation which that person is presenting you.

1) *Think of a person in your life that challenges you emotionally.*

Sit quietly and bring into your mind the person who you feel is challenging you right now. The situation may have occurred in the past, yet you still have emotion around them when the memory of them comes up. It could be your boss, your neighbor, your friend, significant other, ex-wife, ex-boyfriend, etc.

2) *Access the emotional trigger.*

As soon as that person enters your mind, feel into what that person "did to you." Feel it. *What did they do that you are so bothered by? How did they trigger you?* Really get a handle on it. I've got an example in my mind, right now, of someone who has always been extremely judgmental in my life. This person seems to have a judgmental comment about everything, including me.

3) *Recognize the same in you.*

As you think about what this person did, consider how you have manifested that same energy in the world at some point. This requires that you are deeply honest with yourself. Even if what that person did to you was horrible, and you would never in a million years do that to anyone else, you probably are guilty of having at least a thought on par with what that person did to you. If someone violently cut you off, reflect on a time that you have ever had a violent thought towards a person. If violence ever resonates in our body, it creates an energetic flow, which is manifested in the world. In this sense, our violent thoughts are equivalent to another person's violent action. This may sound harsh, but be willing to play with this idea for now and see how it works for you.

Notice that you are not taking blame here for the situation or the actions. You are not condoning what happened or lessening its effect on you. You are also not saying that you are a bad person. You are simply seeing that there may be a bigger picture that is not only personal, but universal.

4) *Repeat the Ho'oponopono Prayer as you remember a time when you held the same energy of that person's action.*

Hold a time in your mind where you manifested back into the world the same or similar energy which you experienced from this person, the same hurt, anger, annoyance, disrespect, whether in thought, deed, or action. Think about yourself as a little child and what happened to you that upset you as you speak the prayer aloud. Apply it to your specific situation. Feel, or see, or hear into your experience as you speak the words. Notice the shifts and release happening.

The following is a sample of a time I used this practice. In my release of a particular person whom I felt was judging me all the time, I had to examine if I have ever been judgmental. Well, I recall once in 1985... I'm kidding. Of course, I've been judgmental – many times. So, I held a picture in my mind of a time when I was exceptionally judgmental. This was my own healing prayer for the judgment I had of another:

"I'm sorry that things happened to me in my life that seemed to force me to use this same energy of judgment as a coping mechanism. I was doing the best I could. I didn't know what else to do and so I reacted.

"I'm so sorry. I'm so sorry that this awful thing happened to me. I'm so sorry that this happened to me. I'm sorry that I expressed judgment in the world in a way that was harmful to myself and others. I'm so sorry that this happened to me, and, the only way I knew how to cope was to express this energy of judgment and its resulting emotions into the world. I'm so sorry. I'm so sorry this happened to me. I'm so sorry that this happened to you, Jenn. Yes. I'm so sorry. I'm sorry this happened to you. I'm so sorry. You didn't deserve it. I'm sorry. The only way you knew how to cope, and, the only way I knew how to cope with this energy was to express this energy of judgment into the world.

"Please forgive me. Please forgive me. Please forgive me for those who I may have hurt through thought, word, or deed by expressing this coping mechanism of judgment into the world. Please forgive me for those who I may have hurt through thought, word or deed. Please forgive me for forgetting that I was innocent. I didn't know better. That's all I could do. Please forgive me for forgetting my innocence. Please forgive me for forgetting that we are all innocent. We are all innocent.

"Please forgive me for forgetting that I am love. I am Divine love. Please forgive me for forgetting that. In that moment, all I could do was cope using

judgment. Please forgive me for forgetting that I am loved and that I am surrounded with love. Please forgive me for forgetting that. Please forgive me for those who I may have hurt through thought, word, or deed. I'm sorry. Please forgive me.

"I love you. I love you for allowing me to go into this and to experience and release this. I love you for the many gifts that I bring to the world. I love you, Jenn. I love you, Jenn, for being you. I love you. I love you. I love you. I love you. I love you.

"Thank you for showing up to show me what I'm ready to work on. I know that you showed up to reveal to me what I'm ready to release in order to achieve the life that I want. Thank you for showing up to reveal to me that I'm ready to forgive; I'm ready to forgive myself.

"Thank you. Thank you. Thank you. Thank you for showing up. Thank you, person who triggered me *[insert name from your personal experience], *for my life. Thank you for the remarkable people who are around me that reflect the joy of who I am. Thank you for my home. Thank you for my life. Thank you for those who I love. Thank you for those who love me. Thank you for the ways that I am exploring and expanding.*

"I'm so sorry. I'm so sorry that I had to experience these things in my life. I'm sorry that the emotions from those experiences got expressed in the world in a way that was challenging. I'm sorry I thought I had to use judgment as a coping mechanism.

"Please forgive me for those who I may have hurt by using this coping mechanism. Please forgive me. Please forgive me. Please forgive me for forgetting that I am innocent, and that we're all innocent and we are all Divine love.

"I love you. I love you. I love you. I love you. I love you. Thank you. Thank you. Thank you. Thank you. Thank you for this moment. Thank you for this clearing. I'm sorry. Please forgive me. I love you. Thank you. I'm sorry. Please forgive me. I love you. Thank you. I'm sorry. Please forgive me. I love you. Thank you. I'm sorry. Please forgive me. I love you. Thank you."

*Use the name of the person whom you felt hurt you to make this experience of forgiveness more real. I also recommend that you use your own name and really dwell in the love you have for yourself.

5) *Allow yourself to feel your negative emotions dissolve into the light of your love.*

Take a deep breath and allow yourself to sit with this new feeling around that person. Allow yourself to feel into the forgiveness that you are feeling now. Sense the release that just happened.

This is a wonderful practice to utilize on a daily basis as we are triggered into trauma so that we don't hold onto it. Sometimes we can't put our finger on what triggered our emotions. It feels as if something just snapped inside of us and, suddenly, we are feeling depressed. These moments are an opportunity to stop, find a way into our self, and notice and pay attention to the cause of these feelings. Choose to clear it in that same moment, rather than feel like a victim. Move through this Spontaneous Transformation process in the form of a prayer to find freedom from that distressing emotion.

Dealing with an Abusive Partner: A Spontaneous Transformation

The following example of clearing and cleansing was taken from a therapeutic session on *MasterWorks Healing Membership Site*. Ramona called in to work through her fear and anger toward her abusive ex-husband who was continuing to terrorize her. As she goes through the process of Ho'oponopono, Ramona examines why she is experiencing this abuse and grapples with how to move toward forgiveness. While you follow along, replace her scenario with one that applies to you and walk through your own releasing process. People often have trouble finding forgiveness when they have been wronged, but without forgiveness we stay locked in the victimization.

"Jennifer, my ex-husband is financially and emotionally abusive. He likes to destroy and terrorize me. He is still trying to do this to me," an intensely speaking Ramona tells me. "He has to finish paying alimony within two months, and he is refusing to do that. He is demanding things that are not his, and lying and threatening me with lawsuits and other things. I feel a tremendous amount of fear because I know he is vindictive. I haven't been able to calm down since yesterday. I am just sitting here shaking as I'm talking to you."

With compassion and empathy, I respond, "Well, that sounds very scary. I think a good way to deal with this is to walk through the Spontaneous Transformation using the Ho'oponopono process. Then move into releasing the initial trauma.

"Before we do that, I think what you are dealing with is so severe that we need to discuss why this is happening, and how life works. This may sound a little bit weird, but we decide in advance, before we come down here, the type of experiences that we want to encounter. I heard Dr. Sue Morter, Master of Bio-Energetic Medicine, say brilliantly that before we come down here, we decide, 'I want a level ten experience of forgiveness,' or 'I want a level ten experience of anger and releasing anger. I want a level ten experience of the opposite of betrayal, which is resolve and empowerment. This is what I want to experience in this lifetime.'

"So, before we even came into this life, when we were on the other side, we asked those around us, 'Can you help me, my friend, down there? Can you help me have a level ten experience of forgiveness in this next lifetime?'

"Interestingly, the people that show up are both our perpetrators and our support. They are our soul group. They've signed up for this assignment. They said, begrudgingly, in some cases, 'Okay, I will be the betrayer. I will be the person that will allow you to experience true forgiveness. I'm in.' There are other people that say, 'I will be there, too, in this capacity.'

"So then the question arises, why in the world would I ask to have this experience? Well, for one, when we're on the other side, we just don't realize the level at which these experiences hurt. Secondly, because it's worth it. It's like asking, why does a dog stick its head out the window and risk getting bugs in its eyes? It's worth the bugs in our eyes. That is why we come down to this planet because the journey and the experience are worth it. There is this beautiful dance that we've agreed to experience in advance. Just knowing this can help provide us with some perspective."

Ramona hears me, but she's positioned in her point of view, "It's almost hard to accept; although, I know exactly what you're saying. I have somewhat of the same belief because I see so much of it in life for everyone. These types of things happen to everyone. We wouldn't be able to have these experiences unless these things happen."

"Exactly," I quickly respond because I can see Ramona is trying to grasp the concept. "Even though these experiences are painful we have a chance to use that cognitive understanding in order to absorb this truth into our consciousness in a deeper way. In fact, right now you are having a body trauma response. It's likely that trauma response started at birth, and that goes for all of us. Early on, a pattern was established that we agreed to experience in this lifetime. As we're born, the pattern is set within our bones and within our body. That pattern then shows up throughout the rest of our life. Yet, the pattern doesn't have to be debilitating after a certain point. When we dive into our lives, we need to own what is happening to us. We need to use that as a point of access into our body and into our soul. This is an opportunity to shift and change that pattern. Continuity of practice will lessen its intensity; especially if this practice is daily and consistent. Literally, we excavate our soul based on what we're experiencing in the moment, and we move into that pattern. We shift the energetic vibration, so the next time that pattern shows up, it's not quite as intense. That pattern, however, is never going to completely go away in this lifetime because that's what we said we wanted to work on or play with."

Ramona quips, "So, I will always be attacked by someone?"

"Not necessarily!" I say, "As you release the need of it as you gain understanding, love, forgiveness, you are coming into a more real experience of yourself and you may just see the pattern in a form that is much easier to manage. The same dynamic may be reflected further outside of you because your energy is no longer resonating that dynamic.

"I used to have something similar happen to me when I would walk down the street in the city. It always seemed the violent, angry homeless guy, not the nice homeless guy, would be the guy that came over to poke me, or yell at me. I would just say to myself, 'Why in a crowd of thousands of people, did this guy choose me?' But I learned to use that for my growth. I asked into it, and I realized it's because I'm vibrationally resonating to a point where he picks it up. It's like they could sniff it. Just like a dog picks up on someone's fear and barks at them. This enflames their past experience. It's just a reminder of what you are here to learn.

"So how do we resolve it? Well, we go into our bodies and we do Ho'oponopono. We take ownership and we forgive ourselves. One of the biggest things we can do for ourselves is forgive ourselves.

"Once we start moving up into the higher vibrating emotions, we just vibrate at a place where we don't experience it. Now, life is still going to show up. We are still on this path which we agreed to walk before we came down here. The patterns are still going to show up, but now we have a level of consciousness that we can bring to it. We have a higher vibrating energy that we bring to the experiences now. So when an incident does show up, we can now look at it and say, 'Wow, I'm ready for that one. Cool.'"

Ramona asks, "How are you able to forgive people? I want to forgive, but I think it is so hard to forgive while the issue is still going on."

I agree, "Oh my god, it's almost impossible, given how loaded the word itself is. Forgiveness has taken on all kinds of meanings from various perspectives. At the end of the day, forgiveness is an experience. Not something you can just say. You can't even demand that of yourself."

"No," says Ramona, "but, I really do want to forgive even though it's still happening. I don't want to be in that energy of not forgiving."

Ramona brings up a remarkable point. You cannot force forgiveness. But you can pray for the willingness to become forgiving. I like to say to the Divine, "God, I am willing. I'm willing. I'm willing. And at this moment, I know I'm not quite able, but I am willing. I'm willing. I know that in *this* moment I'm not able, but I'm willing." That willingness puts me right on the cusp of moving into the higher vibrations. When I'm in a place of feeling those old emotions, experiencing those old behaviors and actions, in that moment, I stop and I just say, "I am willing. I am willing right here, right now. I know that right in this moment, I'm not able, but I'm willing." Willingness, must proceed forgiveness, and moving from anger into willingness is a huge step. Willingness can open the door to something different.

I reassure Ramona that it's okay to admit that she hasn't been able to make it to that space yet.

I say, "The willingness puts us in a place of intention. From there, let's move into some Ho'oponopono. Right now, I want you to think about this man who is really doing some awful stuff. I am actually going to ask you to imagine a time when you've done something similar to someone else. In this case, you've likely never done anything remotely like it. But there may have been a thought, or a minor action, toward someone else at some point in your life that was similar to what he has done to you. I want you to think of those times in your life. Think of the people that are bugging you right now. Think of the times in your life when you may have hurt someone through thought, word, or deed – doing something similar. We're going to start with, 'I'm sorry.' And 'I'm sorry' is a twofold. The first part of it is empathy. I'm sorry for what happened to me. Something happened to me in my life that set up a coping mechanism that created this behavior in the world. I'm so sorry that this thing happened to me in childhood that created a coping mechanism that created a thought and then created a behavior in the world that hurt people.

"I'm so sorry that this happened to me. I'm sorry that something happened to me that created this behavior that showed up in the world. I'm so sorry this happened to me. I'm so sorry. I'm sorry that I didn't realize when I came into human form that this would be so painful. I'm sorry. I'm sorry. I'm sorry that I didn't realize how painful this would be in human form. This stuff happened to me, it created these behaviors, it created this thought, this outreach and this coping mechanism that hurt people. In fact, it hurt some people that I loved, and it hurt some of the people that I didn't like at all, but hurt them, nonetheless. I'm sorry that something happened to me to create this behavior. I'm so sorry that through thought, word, or deed I hurt someone. I'm so sorry."

I proceeded to guide Ramona through her own healing prayer of forgiveness. An attempt to ask Ramona to forgive her ex-husband was unthinkable prior to learning the Spontaneous Transformation. Now Ramona is ready for a breakthrough.

I say directly to Ramona, "This moment of shifting is what you were asking for through the healing prayer. In this space, he showed up to give that release to you. As we do Ho'oponopono whenever we're triggered, we'll start noticing that we don't have to have these big, huge experiences any longer. When we use it in the small moments, when we're cut off in traffic, when someone says something unkind to us, or a stranger says something unkind to us, we put ourselves in a vibrational resonance where we don't have to have these really intense attacks any longer."

"Wow," says Ramona, "So as this goes on in my life, I would imagine that my ex-husband could feel some of this frequency in his life."

"The wonderful bonus about Ho'oponopono," I point out, "is that it actually heals the other person. We take ownership of everyone's stuff because it's a reflection of the energy with us. When we take ownership, then they are shifted into that vibration. I also know that if we all feel into this right now, we can feel that it creates forgiveness for all of us because we're all connected. We're all one. We're all part of the same thing so others experience the shift as well. I have noticed a softening in the other but that cannot be the intention. Instead, it's best for everyone when the focus remains on you."

When the body lets go of the past in the form of judgments, resentments and fears, it also begins to let go of the abusive situation. The self has a chance to live authentically. Just like Dave, Ramona is best to accept her husband for who he is because she cannot change him. The most powerful thing she can do for herself and for him, is to release the anger, pray for willingness, and move toward forgiveness.

Seven

LIVING AUTHENTICALLY and ABUNDANTLY

When something doesn't feel a hundred percent to you and you are trying hard to do what you think you are "supposed" to do, simple tasks feel like you're scaling a steep mountain. If living feels like a struggle most of the time, you are probably pushing against your very nature to live authentically and abundantly. Many of us never take the time to really ask ourselves: *What do we want our lives to be about? What would our day-to-day lives look like if we were true to ourselves?* Instead, we get caught up in the moment trying to put out fires or make rent or pay bills. We don't take the time to listen to our more authentic voice in our body telling us what we are really all about, and what is truly important to us as individuals. When we finally choose to be true to ourselves, and true to what we really want to be in this life, our lives are transformed.

A Self-Loving Path to Transformation

Let me be clear that I am not talking about quitting your corporate job, which you may or may not always enjoy, so that you can climb a mountain to become a guru; or selling your possessions to sail around the world because your relationship is difficult at times and you need your space. You can be true to yourself even if you don't like your job or if you have family challenges.

On the path to being authentic, some of us will throw the baby out with the bathwater. The key word being "path." You don't have to switch overnight. Instead of quitting your well-paying job to be a healer, for example, explore your passions part-time to see if they fit. When you insist that your dream also pay the mortgage, it suddenly becomes an obligation and a big ball of stress. I learned this the hard way.

I could have kept my corporate job and simply changed my energy and attitude around it. I could have found forgiveness around the people at my workplace. Instead, I rebelled against what I felt was *not* me. Whenever we take a kind of stance *against* something, it practically clings to us. Issues came up very quickly to be handled. I experienced extreme stress being close to poverty and enduring two straight years of illness. Of course, a great deal of growth and learning occurred, too. In the end, it all served my path.

Unless you want the accelerated course that comes with a steep learning curve and a whole lot of stress, choose to shift your current circumstance easily and gracefully by beginning with your energy. Since I have taught this gentle, loving path to transformation, I have seen radical changes take place on the outside because someone aligned their internal energy first. I have seen bosses quit, lateral career moves that were fulfilling, and all kinds of other changes that the person could never have anticipated. The point is, you can make your path as difficult or as easy as you want it.

Look at the parts of your life where you feel discontent. See them as opportunities to show up more authentically.

When you change your energy within a circumstance or relationship dynamic, rather than trying to change the circumstance or other person, every aspect of your life can transform from the inside out.

It is our commitment to being authentic that changes our energy. We release so much more of our potential that our abundance increases in every form. Our relationships improve because we bring so much more of our true nature as love to the present. We could be challenged, yet still feel happy and peaceful within because we have a greater perspective of life as being meaningful.

Who Do You Really Want to Be in the World?

Once you understand what is important to you personally, then you can start to feel into how you want to express those values in the world. Once I had taken the time to really tune into my core values, I created a declaration for myself based on how I saw myself living authentically:

"As a conduit and an amplifier, I share mine and others' sacred inspirations and visions on a large scale to encourage and empower shifts in perception for increased global consciousness. In service, I commit to my own growth and the growth of those I interact with, nurturing our unique human potential and creating forgiveness, release, financial abundance and joy along the way. What others see as obstacles, I see as opportunities. I now share my light without hesitation, shining the light of 'the art of life mastery' to all."

This declaration then showed up in all my interactions and decisions. It imbued everything with a beautiful sense of potential for growth. Once I really declared what felt true for me, my purpose became like a lighthouse on an ocean, blinking a guiding light. I steer my boat through the choppy waters of life toward the safety of this shore. I also utilize my core values to guide me when determining which projects I should pursue.

An exploration into living authentically and abundantly requires we conduct an internal excavation to go deeper within to search for what's true for you. Fortunately, these are the type of things we just *know*. We don't know how we know these answers; they just exist inside us. We simply need to take the time to dig beyond the rubble of our daily lives to uncover our true desires which are aligned with our authentic self.

Discover Your Core Self: Practice

1) Use whatever technique takes you deep within and ask yourself: *Who do I want to be in the world?*

Write down all of the answers or clues that arise. This is not the same question as, "What do I want to do or be when I grow up?" Beyond setting specific goals, this is about moving toward your greater intentions in the world. This signifies the place we want to hold and the impact we hope to have on others and in the universe. Do you want to impact just yourself or just your family? These are noble intentions; however, the idea is that you and your purpose are greater than you may now realize. For example, when I took the time to look inside, I realized that my intention was to impact global consciousness. When you go big in your mind and heart, so many more possibilities open up for you and *pull* you forward.

2) Make a list of personal principles and qualities you are drawn to and ask yourself: *What is most important to me?*

Consider what you want your life to feel like: Peace, joy, love, laughter, harmony, magic, abundance, success, elegance, and safety? How might those qualities show up in a life fully lived? List words and sentences that represent the core principles and qualities you want to be and have. When you find the principles and qualities that you came to earth to explore and utilize, you're actually discovering aspects of your purpose.

3) Form a vivid picture of what your life would look like if you embodied these principles and qualities. Then, create a declaration that captures its essence.

Picture a-day-in-the-life of you – what would you be doing if you were authentically guided by those qualities and declaration? What would your day look like? What would your job look like? What should you pursue in order to create these principles? As you go throughout this day, what would your key relationships look like? Begin to shape those words and images into descriptive sentences that form a complete declaration. Make sure it encapsulates your whole essence and purpose.

4) As you embody this declaration, feel into and see how this experience of yourself could impact your experience. Imagine how you want it to manifest.

Close your eyes and feel/sense the change in your body. Feel into the energy of what you want based on your declaration. The more consistently you feel into that reality in your body by creating those vivid images in your mind, the more it will become your reality. As you play with this new energy of what you want, you will create a vibrational resonance with your desires. Once you have created that vibrational resonance, your desires show up, regardless of what your life looks like today. Make it your daily practice to really *feel* that at least once a day for longer and longer periods. Create this picture on a regular basis.

For example, after I created my declaration of my core principles and qualities, I was able to see, sense, and feel my life in a much clearer way. My coaching practice very quickly started to show up and I was asked to be a speaker in several new thought churches locally. Joe Vitale heard about my work, sought me out, and asked me to be in his book, *The Key*. Seriously, these opportunities showed up without struggle or pushing. I declared my intention and it occurred as I was ready.

Now, this is not to say that you can sit in your bedroom and meditate all the time, and then – wham – you get what you want. Joe Vitale didn't just send me an email out of the blue. Instead, I engaged him in a conversation through the work that I was doing. I took that step forward because it was already the truth of who I was within myself. Eventually, he heard about me, then sought me out. Depending on how far away you are now from living authentically, there could be a huge deal of action that goes into creating the life that is aligned with your truth.

If you push yourself beyond what you are resonating with, you can burn yourself out and give up too easily, saying, "This stuff doesn't work." When you use this daily practice of centering into your core self, your combined energy and actions attract those opportunities by using people of like energy.

You will know you are resonating with your authentic self when things come more easily to you and beautiful synchronicities occur more often.

Living As the Authentic Self: A Spontaneous Transformation

The intent of Spontaneous Transformation is to help the participant to live a more authentic life, accepting greater possibilities that would create more wealth and happiness.

As Liz describes, "I've been trying to figure out what it is in my past that may be blocking me in my current situation. I've had a hard time coming up with an answer because I don't believe I had a childhood trauma or anything like that. I just realized that I am coming from the standpoint that everything I earn is a result of really hard work. Just before this morning, I realized that maybe what's blocking me is somewhat of a resentment, which is a huge word, but a resentment that I might have with my husband. When I had my child, I wanted to stay home and raise her, but I feel like he never gave me the permission to be a stay-at-home mom. I've always earned over two-thirds of the household income. So he always had this requirement that I had to work. Funny how the universe works, I feel like I've manifested the situation of 'having to work really hard.' I had worked for years at this company, and I was finally ready to quit, but before I got around to it, I got laid off. So I got my wish there. Then I went and opened up a business, but my partnership didn't work. Now I'm trying to figure out what is next.

"I've learned my lesson. Whatever I do next, I want it to be something that I really want to do, that I really love to do, that I'm inspired to do. I'm trying to figure out what that really is. And I admire the declaration that you had. I kind of want to get to that point. But I'm just wondering how to do that. I'm not really earning an income right now, and have a lot of challenges meeting the household bills because my husband's income, although he is providing, has never been enough. So, I'm in a situation where I'm taking out home equity loans to pay for the mortgage. I don't feel like I'm making any progress."

After listening, I reply, "I think I got it, Liz. I laughed a little bit at the beginning when you said you didn't have any childhood trauma."

Liz not understanding says, "I couldn't think of one."

I back off saying, "That's fine. But you were born, right?"

Liz suspiciously says, "Yes."

I clarify, "That's a trauma. What I hear is we've got provider stuff here: 'I have to work really hard to earn.' There's some resentment here because of the perception that your husband has forced you to keep working. There's the issue of there not being enough income coming in, but you're happy with the layoff."

Liz admits, "Yes. I just saw it as a huge opportunity because I had planned to leave the company no matter what. And it came six months before I got a chance to do that with almost a full year of salary."

Inquisitively, I ask, "How long ago was that, Liz?"

Liz answers, "Several years ago."

I restate, "So now you're looking to work at something you love."

"I really wanted to get into helping people spiritually," Liz declares.

I ask, "Do you have any training in any way in that field?"

"No, I don't," conceded Liz, "That's why I'm starting to look into to what it is that I should be doing."

Politely pointing out the conflict of beliefs to Liz, I say, "There is a big chasm right now between your beliefs and your actions.

"I will give you an example. Right now, I firmly believe that no matter what I put in my mouth, I shouldn't gain weight. So, I think I should be able to eat anything. Unfortunately, there is a big chasm between my intellectual beliefs, and my true sense of knowing that. My knowing part goes, 'I don't think so.' So, until my knowing part catches up with my belief, it isn't going to happen. My ice cream diet is not going to be successful.

"We do the same thing in our life. We see something that we want, and we push out into the world and say, 'I want that.' Then we expect it to pay our mortgage. There are actually steps between an intention and receiving that intention. One of the things that I say a lot is, 'I don't recommend that your dreams pay your mortgage.' It puts way too much pressure on your dreams, and they are no longer your dreams as a result.

"From a practical perspective, to start, do work that you can make an income from to take the pressure off the family. That would be my first recommendation. I had to do the same thing. I was a healer for eighteen years, but I only did it part time, and I never thought I could make an income from it, which is why I worked in corporate America for many years. Eventually, I quit corporate America thinking I'm ready to live my dream. My sense of knowing had not caught up with my unconscious belief that I could make money doing what I love with passion.

"So I had to go back to doing marketing. I had to go backwards. But it was different this time. I now thought of it as a stepping-stone toward making the income I needed at the time, so I was closer. I could then open the energetic space to receive my dreams.

"There are lots of people that say, 'I want to do what I love.' Great! Hold that intention with all your might, and don't put the expectation that it's going to pay your mortgage because it will create too much density to hold the etheric state of a dream.

"As I worked as a marketer, which provided me a comfort zone, I started building my healing practice. I did that for almost a year. I was taking my dream and putting it into action piece by piece by holding the intention. I remember when my last marketing client released me. I didn't hate it even though I hated it before. I can use the word hate because I did earlier. That's why I left it. I hated it. I didn't like doing it anymore. I was done with it. But I didn't hate it for that year because I was so grateful for the opportunity to work at something that gave me a good income to pay my bills. I held it within the greater perspective of serving my declaration. I was in a job I didn't like with gratitude holding the intention for my dream and taking action to move it forward.

"This job allowed me to have the space to be open to Divine inspiration. Divine inspiration drops in when we are in that place of openness. This inspiration gave me several different, huge business ideas which are now generating tremendous income for me and allowed me to drop that other occupation. Yet, the skills it provided me still serve me in living more authentically and abundantly.

"So I want you to feel into your body. What does it feel like in your body right now as I tell you all this?"

"I don't know what it is," lamented Liz, "but right at the bottom of my head, behind my throat, I've been carrying a heavy feeling that I just can't shake."

"Let's bring that energy into place," I continue to say, "We all want what we want now! Wanting to do what you love is a good thing, but you have to go about that practically; meaning in alignment with how the universe works. Right now, as I say that, Liz, describe the energy in the back of your head."

Liz begins by saying, "It feels like the heaviness is going upwards in my head."

Probing I ask, "Does it feel like if you apply for a job that you are being inauthentic to yourself?"

"Exactly," answers Liz.

"Here is the reality," I say as I lay it out on the table, "You are already authentic right now, no matter what you are doing for a living. There is nothing inauthentic about participating in your own family's income.

I recently was talking to my friend who you've heard me talk about before, Mary A. Hall, about what it would be like for me to go back into corporate America right now. I realized that I would be a completely different person in corporate America now because of the shifts and changes that I've experienced over the last few years. My level of confidence is higher. This is predicated on not the fact that I am doing what I love, but because I've done the work within myself through modes such as Spontaneous Transformation to be more authentic with myself; therefore, showing up in the world differently. This means that being in the world is about my beingness and not dependent on what I do. What I do is irrelevant to my authenticity of being and that is where the personal freedom comes in. What we attract, as a result, matches that higher vibration. I can actually feel your body beginning to get this concept and opening up. Is my sense true for you?"

Relieved for words to explain her confusion, Liz eagerly agrees.

"So right now, at the base of your skull, there is a place that is grappling with this notion that you're somehow betraying yourself by moving back into corporate America," as I restate the conflicted belief to Liz, I continue, "I want to tell you now, that belief is not true. What does that feel like when I tell you that?"

Liz exhales as if to feel into that energy in her head and proceeds to answer, "My head is beginning to feel lighter."

"Liz, I also want to add, that being a healer means you can bring your light wherever you are, even if it's Corporate America," I say. "This doesn't mean that you're going to go in there as this marauding guru. That just means you're going to go in there as this beautiful, authentic being. You're going to model what it feels like to be an authentic being. This doesn't have to be your long-term destiny. But knowing you can go in there and be authentic allows you to create the space for money and brand new opportunities to come in that you haven't imagined yet. This action allows you to create the space where Divine inspiration and Divine ideas come in. Then you can continue to take inspired action on that which might take you down a different path.

"The other thing that I want you to know is that when we say, 'I can't do that thing over there because I hate it, I don't like it, I don't want it,' that energy sets up its own energetic vibration.

"I just want your body to feel what it's like to stay with this new concept here that we are discussing in our Spontaneous Transformation work. What does it feel like in your head right now that we talked about this fact that you could go back to corporate America?"

Liz answers with a sparkle that she hasn't had since she began this session with me, and says, "Actually pretty good. I feel a tingling all the way down my arm. My head feels a lot lighter."

"Can you feel your authentic self?" I ask.

Liz responds, "I don't know what it feels like to feel my authentic self, so I'm having some difficulty feeling that."

"Fair enough," I say. "Let's just pretend right now that you can be your authentic self. Let's just pretend. Then we can go back to wherever you were before. So we're just going to pretend in this moment you're feeling your authentic self. What does that feel like?"

"It's tingling all the way to the tip of my toes, and all the way up my legs. There is energy moving in my body," Liz answers with delight.

"Now bring your energy into the center of your being and kind of drop your shoulder blades down your back. Allow that to just open up in your whole being," I say as I feel into her whole body opening up.

Liz describes, "Wow. It's just a little vibration all throughout my body."

"Now this is the space that we imagine the feeling state of our future reality," as I set up the visualization for Liz, I say, "I want you to just imagine that it is six months from now. That beautiful, authentic body you have right now, in this moment, is at the office expressing this authenticity in everything you do. Do you see how powerful you are? Do you see the opportunities you manifest? Do you see the people around you who are kind of looking at you going, 'She's got some kind of secret sauce that I would like some of?'"

Liz interjects with enthusiasm, "I'm just radiating the energy."

"You got it," I say, "Now, I can feel you wanting to move on. That's part of *your* pattern. What I would really like for you to do is to notice over the next couple of weeks how you want to move on. Being authentic really is about being present and fully embracing this moment. The feeling of 'moving on,' which is part of your pattern, is also the opposite of abundance in many ways because it's an energy of grasping toward what's next, where we say, 'Okay, give me what's next! I've got to get me what's next.'"

Liz agrees, "Yes, I've had that pattern my whole life over many things."

"Just feel right now, this is your opportunity, right in this moment, to feel its opposite," I instruct, "Just be present in this moment and feel what it feels like to be authentic in your body. The moving-on piece could be envisioning how authenticity shows up in your life in the future. Do you feel that there's no need to go to what's next?"

Liz affirms.

"Wrapping up here Liz," I say, "when you're in that place of the now moment, 'what's next' shows up anyway. Do you see how that happens? That's an example of what creative beings we are. When we come to this place, the next thing shows up. It just shows up because we are in a place of trusting, not questioning."

As we all learn to live in closer alignment with our true values and embody the qualities we hold dearest to us, our bodies feel the shift. If we have been holding onto physical manifestations that don't coexist well with our new vision for our life, those troubling areas may resurface to be realigned.

As wondrous possibilities open up before you now, you will have the chance to take care of your body in a new way. You may see old health issues in a new light. Your greater understanding will prepare you to move beyond them, if that is your choice.

Eight

RESOLVING HEALTH ISSUES

Sickness and disease are an integral part of the human experience. Sickness is a language our body utilizes to get our attention. Where there is pain and disease there is opportunity to grow beyond who you think you are into who you really are. You can expand your energy and current understanding beyond the bounds of what poses constraints on your freedom and fullest enjoyment of life. As with all other experiences, it is there to teach you. Look directly into it. Love it. Forgive it. It is all a journey into you. Within the universe there is nothing that is *not* you. So whatever symptoms are showing up, you can even gain awareness of your oneness with that too, and thereby choose to hold onto it or release it.

Health issues also provide a path to leave the planet. We have not "lost" if we pass on. Death is part of the Divine dance. We are truly not getting out alive. Even if we believe in ascension, the body that has ascended is not the three-dimensional body we have now. It is not, in our human terms, "alive." However, it does change. We live to grow and that still holds true in our time of passing. The body is in a constant state of transformation. Here, you have the opportunity to learn more about the places where the body and mind merge, so that you can better partner with them on its path.

Where the Body and Mind Merge

That may be hard to hear if you are in pain right now or your body seems to be taking you down a path that is *not* of your choosing. The idea may even make you feel angry or annoyed, so use that. Your emotional, mental and physical activities are all connected. They can serve as your access point to connect and dialogue with your body in a very immediate way.

When pain is so severe and immediate, being present to possibilities long enough to hear what the body is trying to tell us can be challenging. Pain certainly captures our attention and directs it to those places which have needs. It can sap our energy, but it also brings up vibrational energies and emotions to be explored. We are in a partnership with our body because there is, in effect, no separation between the mind and the body as evidenced through all the Spontaneous Transformation sessions throughout this book. We can observe that the body's experience in the moment is actually fluid and dynamic. This is always true, yet some of our stuff sticks around because we are not changing vibrationally. We are holding it in place. If you look at each session, you see that the recipient is always able to transform their physical and emotional experience/sensation by: 1) directing their attention, 2) asking what that aspect needs, and 3) providing it vibrationally. It is a straightforward process. We do it every day. When we are thirsty, we reach for a beverage. When we are uncomfortable, we shift in our chair. When we are lonely, the body seeks companionship.

> *The body is constantly speaking to us about its physical and emotional needs. We gain insight and fulfill its requirements. This same process holds true when we face physical conditions.*

We need to be just as willing to listen and serve the body's needs. Spirit is matter in 3-D. Spirit partners with matter and matter is our body. The body is then our partner as the material part of our experience. Our bodies are here as beautiful, supportive systems to respond to that which we brought with us to play. The "challengers" that come along then – betrayers, lovers, parents, friends, people we collide with in our cars, disease and health issues – whatever the experience of stress, are felt on the physical in a range of ways. We can then use the body as part of this juicy life adventure for our growth.

When symptoms arise, we often ignore their whispers, their recommendations for changes in our lifestyle or our thought processes. We act as if there is nothing we can do, as if the body has a mind of its own and it has betrayed us. The key is to remember that you and your body share the same mind. It is yours to use as you will.

Why then do we sometimes ignore those whispers until they become cries and our body shuts down? We push through the messages that say, "Rest, eat better, please go out and take that walk up the hill!" It's the same reason we repress difficult emotions. We think that dealing with the lessons will be painful. Perhaps. But not as painful as when they are ignored so long that they enter the body as disease and hurt. We push and repress until these things show up in our body as health issues. This is the Compression Theory again in action. When we don't listen, the volume/pain or discomfort/manifestation of the illness increases to get our attention!

Listen. That is the first simple step. Because the body and mind are so intimately and inextricably related, it is vitally important, when facing difficulties with our health, to dialogue with our body in order to tap into our body's natural healing abilities. In fact, the body is attempting to reflect back to you what you are holding onto in your consciousness. It offers wonderful expressions of our beliefs and traumas. It is there FOR us, not against us. It is always in full support, simply responding to the conditions and signals you give it.

The following three sessions are taken from the *MasterWorks Healing Membership Site*. Each participant is grappling with some form of sickness, disease, or chronic pain. As you read through the following therapeutic sessions, replace the callers' experience with a body issue that you, too, are struggling with. Journeying through the dialoguing process with others always reveals to us the universal nature of our existence, even if you have a different ailment. That is why we can learn and grow as we follow along while others develop a closer relationship with their bodies on their personal path to perfect health.

Thyroid Issues: A Spontaneous Transformation

"I was wondering if we could work on my tremors," states Sara.

"Tremors," I restate. "Are you on any medication?"

"No," replies Sara.

"So you don't take any prescription medication at all?" I inquire again.

"I take medication for thyroid," answers Sara.

"So, that's where it's coming from," I point out.

Sara questions, "It is?"

"Yes," I affirm. "There's nothing wrong with the medication. It's just that it's triggering something. Just feel into that and see if that's true for you. Is this true for you?"

"No," demands Sara.

"What's the first answer that pops into your mind when I ask you what is causing the tremors?" I ask.

Sara slightly defensive responds, "My mind is telling me it's more from my cervical spine somewhere."

"Sara, I keep getting thyroid," going with my gut, I say, "let's just hang out with your thyroid for a minute. Just tell me what it looks like in your thyroid?"

"Nothing is coming up," Sara blankly answers.

"Let's take a minute and put your hand on your heart. Bring your attention into your heart," as I pause while talking. "That's it. If you want, tap a heartbeat on your heart. We're going to bring ourselves into our body. Just feel a little tapping. Thump-thump… thump-thump… Slow it down. Good. Now imagine that there's a nose in your heart, and it's breathing for you. That's it. Next, bring your attention fully into your body. Do you think you're in your body, Sara?"

"Probably," a disconnected Sara answers. "I'm almost never in my body."

"Would you mind if we do a little play session, like a fantasy session?" knowing I need to reshift her focus, I continue, "This session is not real life. It is a hundred percent pretend. Are you willing to play?"

"Yes, I'll pretend," Sara complies.

"Very good." Noticing her resistance easing up, I say, "I don't know if you noticed the shift in energy just by saying, 'I'll pretend.' There is a little bit more freedom and breath in there. Can you notice that at all?"

Sara still completely disconnected to her physical experience says, "No."

"That's okay," I move forward saying, "So, we're in pretend land. We're pretending just like we used to when we were four and five, right? Just pretend. What would it be like if you were in your body? Just pretending, just kind of imagining."

"If I were in my body, I would probably be very peaceful," says Sara. "It would be calming and quiet."

I restate, "Calming and quiet, that is good. Allow yourself to feel that calm and quiet. I want you to just pretend that it's two years from now, and you've had two full years of being in your body, really in your body, and feeling this peace and calm and quiet. Two years down the road, tell me, what does your life look like?"

Sara following along with the pretending responds, "Joyful."

I ask her to describe, "What happens when you wake up in the morning two years from now, after being in your body and feeling this peace and calm every day? What does it feel like as you open your eyes? What's the first thing that happens?"

"I can't wait to get up," says Sara.

Knowing we are getting somewhere I encourage Sara by saying, "Yes. So feel that. Allow that in. 'I can't wait to get up.' Right. So what does your day look like? What kind of things are you doing in this life? It's likely quite different than it is now. Is that true?"

Sara now fully engaged in the pretending says, "Yes. I get up and I get ready for work. I'm excited to go to work, and it's not going to stress me out."

Catching the subtlety of the negative self-talk I say, "Let's put that in the way it really feels. There were some 'nots' in there like, 'I'm not going to...'

"So what does it really feel like without limitation? Remember this is two years from now. Again, we're completely playing. And you're getting ready for work. What does it feel like in your body as you're anticipating and excited and enthusiastic about going in to work? Again, we're pretending here, right?"

"It would be joyful," declares Sara. "I would have expectations about having a great day."

Guiding Sara in the process now that she's relaxed enough to play along, I say, "Yes. Feel that. Now you're at work. Again, we're in complete fantasyland. So it may not be the same job. Or it may be. Your job will be with a bunch of people who are really in vibrational alignment with peace, calm and quiet. Imagine that this could actually be fun. You don't have to even see the people right now. Just feel the essence of the people that are there in support of you, acknowledging you, appreciating you. You, in turn, are acknowledging and appreciating them. Now, watch how you show up within this environment. Feel your power within this environment. What's really cool is that all this was created by you through being simply peaceful, calm, and quiet as a result of being in your body."

Excitedly Sara interjects with the hope of possibility in her future and says, "It feels great."

"Yes," affirming Sara's hope, I continue, "We just played a little trick on your mind. We showed your mind what was possible. You're mind, or ego, has been protecting you. It thought that you needed to be protected from your body. Now we just showed your mind what's possible if you're in your body. I want you to know that right now your mind knows this. Your mind now understands how valuable this process is for you. Your mind loves you. All your mind/ego ever wants to do is protect you. That's it. We just embrace that beautiful mind for wanting to protect you.

"Your mind wants to protect you. It wants you to be safe. In the past, it wasn't safe to be in your body. So your mind said, 'Okay, we're not going to go there because it doesn't feel safe.' We just showed your mind that your beautiful body is actually the safest place on the planet. Your body has all the answers, has all the intuition, has all the knowledge you need to create this life that you just experienced.

"I'm going to have a conversation with your mind, right now.

"'Beautiful mind, thank you. Thank you for protecting Sara so perfectly and beautifully. You listened really carefully, and you heard that it wasn't safe to be in her body. Now we've shown you what's possible when she's in her body. It's the ultimate safety. It's the wonderful place of safety.'

"So, Sara, what does it feel like in your body right in this moment?"

As a gentle silence ensues, Sara responds, "Quiet."

I ask, "Sara, are you in your body?"

Sara answers, "Yes."

I ask, "Sara, are we in fantasyland or are we in your body right now?"

Sara answers, "I am in my body."

I remind Sara by saying, "Let's thank your beautiful body.

"'Thank you for sticking around even though I wasn't there for so long. There are great reasons why I left you-my body – great reasons. I left you – my body – to protect myself. We thank the systems of my soul for creating that scenario, that coping mechanism. It was perfect, but now the opposite is true. Now, it's actually safer for me to be fully present inside of you – my body. You're all grown up, and you have a beautiful body that's here to protect you. You have a mind that loves you and understands now how perfect it is to be in your body. Now, I want you to just kind of hang out with the thyroid for a moment. What does it look like in that beautiful thyroid?'"

"I'm not very visual," states Sara.

"That's okay, Sara," I respond. "You have other senses that you may be more inclined to use. Can you tell me what you feel? What do you sense when you hang out with the thyroid area, which happens to be right at the base of your cervical spine?"

"The first word that came to my mind was stiff," answers Sara.

"Yes, stiff," I repeat. "Let's just say, thank you, thyroid, for sharing that. We're going to just ask that beautiful thyroid what it needs. We understand that it has been stiff. What does it need around this stiffness? Is there anything else it needs to share with us about this stiffness?"

"More flexibility," responds Sara.

"What would more flexibility look and feel like?" I ask.

"Being more in the flow and not being so stuck," Sara answers.

"The thyroid is part of the endocrine system, and plays a very big role in the adrenals and the ovaries. It also regulates the chemistry of the body and the metabolism of the body. There is a shift happening right now as we just kind of feel what it would feel like to be flexible," I explain.

Sara quiped, "Less judgmental."

"Less judgmental of who?" I inquire for more.

"Myself, primarily," answers Sara.

"I want you to tell me the first thing that comes into your mind about that voice of judgment." I say.

"I think it's my ego," answers Sara.

"No, I don't think so," I explain, "I usually don't say 'no,' but it feels like someone from the past is the voice of judgment that got stuck in your thyroid.

Sara answers, "My mother."

"We're just going to look at your mom," I instruct, "I want you to bring yourself to the kid, to the child that is being judged by your mom. How old were you when it was at its worst?"

"It always seemed to be bad," Sara reflects, "I don't know. I would say I was always in a rage with my younger sister, I was maybe around six."

"Bring your attention to that six-year-old that was you," I instruct. I want you to really be present for her. Let's pretend this is two years from now, and you have been living in peace and calm, okay?"

"Okay," says Sara.

"Bring the present you, which is peaceful and calm, to the six-year-old," I say. "That six-year-old now feels the full force of this beautiful, peaceful, calm, empowered you. I want you to feel, and get a sense of, what that six-year-old is feeling as she feels your support and love and presence for her."

Sara following along says, "She feels more nurtured."

"Yes. It just hasn't been a feeling that's familiar for her," I explain. "She's opening up like a flower to the sunshine of your attention. Yes, feel that.

"Allow her to really experience that presence and support. Ask her to share with you what's going on, what is happening. What happened? The words don't matter as much as the essence. You're just being present for the essence of what she is sharing with you. She is telling you a big, long involved story about what happened, and there are probably some tears there. You're just a hundred percent present for her, listening intently. Is that happening?"

"Yes," says Sara.

"Good," moving on, I say. "Now, she's sharing, and she's upset. You're present. She feels completely heard. Good. And what's happening now? Are you kind of holding her?"

Sara describes, "I'm just feeling like I mattered."

"Yes, that's true," I repeat, "that's true. You did matter. Now, we're going to turn around, and we're going to look at your mom. Your mom can't see you. We're going to look right at her. We can see her up close. It's like we have a cloak of invisibility around us. She can't see you, or hear us, but you can see her very, very clearly.

"I want you to just notice the tension in her body. Notice the places of holding in her body. I want you to notice that just right behind her heart there is a big ball of light. This ball of light is her sacred chamber. We all have it. No matter who we are, every single person on the planet has a sacred chamber that is a Divine connection to source energy. Do you see hers?"

"Yes," says Sara.

"Now, I want you to notice something else. As you notice her sacred chamber, you also probably notice, or sense, the places of restriction, maybe a little bit of sludge. Similar to how your thyroid feels, but there is quite a bit of it all through her body. Do you see that?" I repeat, "Do you sense that?"

"Yes," says Sara.

"I want you to know that every single time she said anything to you, and just pretend that you can see the mechanism of this, it started in light," I say. "It started in that place of love. Do you see that?"

"Yes," says Sara.

"Everything she said to you started there. It started with good intentions. Then as it made its way through the entire trauma and all the sludge and all the places of tension and stiffness, it showed up in the world as something other than pure love," then I ask, "Is that true?"

Sara responds from the deepest most relaxed place of trusting that I have witnessed from her during our session with a big, "Yes."

"Every time she said anything to you in the form of judgment, it started from a place of love but got convoluted as it filtered through these traumas in her own body," I ask, "Do you see that?"

Sara answers, "Yes."

"I want you to really understand," I explain, "I especially want the six-year-old to understand that it had nothing to do with you and everything to do with her distorted filter. That judgment was hers from that perception. Her judgment likely got held in her body from someone else, just as her judgment got stuck in your thyroid. Do you see the patterning?"

Sara says, "Yes."

I ask, "How does the six-year-old feel now that she sees her mom's intention was always from a place of love?"

Sara answers, "Understanding."

"It feels like there can be some breath there," I state. "Both of you, your little one and the grown up version of you, take a nice deep breath. That's it. Now, just give your beautiful little one a hug. Show your little one that you are still present now even though her mom wasn't really able to support her because of this stuff that she was holding onto, and, no matter what she needs, you're always there for that little girl.

"After this session, I would like you to grow her up. I would like your little girl to grow to eight and to ten and twelve and fifteen and eighteen and twenty-two, and to whatever, until she's your age. See what each age feels like from her perspective, what her life would be like with this new confidence, with this new sense of 'I mean something. I get that my mom was doing the best she could, and I mean something.' Do you get a sense of that?"

Sara says, "I do."

"Begin by feeling what it feels like to be peaceful, calm, and quiet and in your body," knowing now that Sara is really getting a grasp of this being in your body concept. I continue, "We're going to allow this little girl to have that same experience as she grows up. You might notice that you go to a different school and have different friends. You might even have different relationships. You're re-patterning your life into this new energy. The body doesn't know the difference. It's a story that allows the body to resonate at this new level. This allows your little girl to grow up to be you, this confident, powerful, peaceful, calm and quiet being of light and love. How is the thyroid doing now?"

"Great," Sara says.

I wrap up by saying, "As you practice this exercise regularly, you may need to adjust your thyroid medication. In six weeks, or so, you may want to go to the doctor and just get everything checked out. Listen to the recording of our session again and go through the feelings. Create this peaceful, calm, quiet energy within your body. Then grow your little girl up. Commit to this practice of re-patterning for fifteen minutes every day. Can you commit to fifteen minutes every day?"

Through Sara's discipline to practicing the re-patterning through Spontaneous Transformation, not only was she able to eliminate her thyroid medicine completely under the supervision of her doctor, the stiffening in her back near the thyroid also eased up.

Fibromyalgia Issues: A Spontaneous Transformation

Wendy explains, "Basically, I have been dealing with symptoms that are similar to fibromyalgia for years. I've done a lot of personal work. I've done a lot of facilitated work. I've got one area, mostly on the top of my shoulders and radiating up into my head, that I'm pretty certain is partially gunk from trauma."

I respond, "Wendy, it's all gunk from trauma, honey."

Wendy agrees, "Yes. We had a little bit of trauma on the side."

I ask, "What kind of job do you or did you have?"

Wendy answers, "I do massage therapy," and adds, "I had a lot of little symptoms that were dismissed over time."

"So you've been a massage therapist?" trying to lock specifics, I ask.

"Yes," Wendy answers, "I used to do that."

I probe, "What do you do now?"

"I am working to get myself off of disability, so that I can be self-employed and independent once again," Wendy explains.

Getting the picture more clearly, I say, "Now, you really need your body to be a massage therapist, and fibromyalgia is antithetical to that, isn't it?"

Wendy says, "Yes."

I start the Spontaneous Transformation process with Wendy by saying, "Let's take a little journey. Wendy, right in this moment, let's do the heartbeat. I want you to tap your heart like a thump-thump with your fingers. Tap on your chest. There we go. Take a nice, deep breath. I want you to kind of sense and look across the room. I want you to see the objects that are in the room. I want you to say to yourself, 'That object is over there and I'm here.' There it is. There we go. 'I am here. I am here.'"

The reason I do this with clients is to get them into their Now Self. By identifying an object and identifying themselves, I am moving them out of their head and into the presence of their body.

"Now, feel the objects across the room. I want you to feel the space between you and the objects," as I restate, then ask Wendy to tune into, "'There is the object over there, and I'm here.' Feel the space in between. Pretend that your heart has a nose and it's slowing the breath down.

It's breathing in. It's breathing out. There we go. You can feel the presence now?"

Wendy answers, "Yes."

"Now, first of all," I say to Wendy, "this is something that you will want to do every day. As you bring your attention fully into your heart, and see the objects across the room. Say, 'They are over there, and I am here.'"

Wendy says, "I am here."

"Good," I affirm. "Now, bring your energy into your heart. Just below your heart, I want you to notice that there's a sacred chamber. Bring your attention into your sacred chamber. Yes, there you are. As you bring your attention into your sacred chamber, can you feel a kind of atmospheric shift and change that happens as you move inside there?"

Wendy says, "Yes, I'm getting tingles."

I say to Wendy, "If you did that every day and just hung out there for a few minutes in your sacred chamber that alone would go a long way. Going inside your body would allow your body's natural healing abilities to be reanimated.

"As you're feeling this place, feel into your sacred chamber. Feel how powerful and connected you are. Is that true? Those are the words I'm getting. Is that true?"

Wendy answers, "Yes, definitely."

I ask, "Do you feel how powerful you are in this place?"

"Yes," Wendy says with a sense of empowerment.

"There it is. Right there." I say as I point out the presence of being in the moment. "How does that feel being fully connected and in the moment?"

"Really good," Wendy responds.

"Isn't being fully present in the moment great?" I ask.

Wendy states, "Yes, my solar plexus and heart are exchanging energies."

Giggling I add, "I feel like there is a giggle there. Can we go with that for a moment? Join me, Wendy, in releasing a giggle. Just follow my giggle."

Something very powerful for me about doing the giggling exercise... Our bodies are so amazing. We release energy when we cry, but we underestimate the energy that is set free when we giggle.

After laughing for a minute or two, I compose myself and ask Wendy, "Did you feel that release? Did you feel your shoulders just open up?"

Wendy, still giggling says, "Yes."

"Your homework," I say, "is to bring your attention into your body through the heart and bring your attention into the sacred chamber, then hang out in the sacred chamber. It doesn't have to be a long time, but it should be every day. I would actually recommend doing it morning and night. That's going to go a long way by allowing your body to feel grounded and allowing the natural healing abilities of the body to take over. Just being in your body is a really important part because it's hard to be in your body when you're in pain. Fibromyalgia is very uncomfortable. It's just saying, 'I don't want to be here. I don't want to be in my body, and I'm completely overwhelmed with three dimensions.' That's fibromyalgia. So by bringing your attention in through your heart, then into your sacred chamber, you're actually deep within the deepest connection of your being. You're deep within your body, and you've kind of allowed yourself to go to the core. From the core, the healing can expand outward."

Most the time when we are uncomfortable with pain or a chronic issue, we do the opposite that needs to be done. We avoid being present in our body. In order to move the energy blockages that keep us in discomfort, we actually need to be present and feel through the pain. We identify it, feel it, and breathe through it, and in Wendy's case, we giggled through it. It's no wonder they say, "Laughter is the best medicine."

Cancer Issues: A Spontaneous Transformation

As Miriam describes, "I've been having some health and physical challenges for the last seven months. It feels like one thing after the other. It's either a health issue or an injury or expensive mechanical thing breaking down and stuff. I just don't know where to go with it or what to do."

Listening for the relevancy of information I ask, "You said it's been seven months?"

Miriam confirms.

Inquisitively I ask, "What happened seven months ago?"

Miriam answers, "I was diagnosed with breast cancer, and I had a lumpectomy and then radiation."

"That's a pretty big deal," I say, "How is it going?"

"Fine," Miriam says unmoved, "It looks like everything is clear. I'm psychically feeling like everything is clear."

"Yes, it feels right to me, too, but it was a big shock?" I ask, checking in.

Miriam cops to the fact that it was extremely shocking.

"Big shock." I affirm, "Mortality is in your face. How old are you?"

Miriam answers, "Sixty-five."

"You don't seem like sixty-five," I observe and ask, "Do you feel sixty-five?"

"Thank you and no," says Miriam, "Except when I'm feeling injured and I'm in pain or can't walk very well."

"Yes, that can change with Spontaneous Transformation," I state. "How's your weight, nutrition, self-care, and all of that stuff?"

"My nutrition is good," Miriam says, but counters with, "I probably need to lose forty or fifty pounds."

"That's something you are going to want to take a look at," I say with emphasis, "I'm on a new bent with this myself. I have about the same amount of weight to lose. I'm working on some new nutritional habits, and I honestly haven't felt this good in years. I'll explain what is going on for me, and maybe you can relate.

"Several things are happening for me. One of the things is, I used to drink a glass of wine about five, six nights a week. It was my transition into relaxation. So, as I finished my day, I would stop working, and then have a glass of wine in order to transition into not working. What I realized is that the wine was turning things off within my body and within my mind. For the first two weeks that I stopped this habit, I dealt with emotions that I was turning off prior to that, feelings of being overwhelmed, upset, and anxious.

"Sometimes we use food, we use alcohol, and we use sugar, in particular, to repress the energies that are trying to bubble up in the consciousness. Sugar is a total addiction, by the way.

"It's ironic, really, that I teach what I most need to learn. I move through the world talking about using everything, using the moments of trigger, and, yet, I was using a habit of repression. The compression theory, then, is you repress it, you repress it, you repress it... it gets bigger and bigger and bigger, until something shows up. Normally, what shows up is a health issue. For me, it was adrenal exhaustion.

"The other thing I've learned, Miriam, is that our body is our partner. I have been denying that partnership with my body and pushing through. Many women do this, too; we push through. Men do it, too, but women seem to bring it into a new art form and push through even if we're not up to it.

"The opportunity for us now, all of us now, is to change those habits. Health issues show up to tell us that something needs to change. So, Miriam, unless you've changed things quite dramatically after that cancer incident, then other things are going to keep showing up. It's the compression theory.

"Basically, the body says, 'I want you to listen, and I want you to listen NOW. I want you to make some changes. I want you to pay attention to me, I'm your body. I want you to listen to me, I'm your body. I want you to be in partnership with me.'

"Now I have to listen very carefully and ask, 'Will what I'm about to eat work for me in this moment be in my best interest?' Sometimes something will work for me in one moment, and, three hours later, it won't. But, I'm listening, I'm in partnership, and I'm honoring my body. I'm realizing that my body is here as an absolute, beautiful, sacred, foundation. My body is here as support for me to move my vision into the world.

"It's important to get a handle on the fact that our bodies are a place of absolute sacred perfection, and we need to actually support our body. Emotions are half of the equation, and the other half of the equation is nutrition and listening and letting our bodies tell us what they need. With that, let's just take a look and move inside our bodies. Bring your attention to your heart. Put your hand on your heart, and just tap a bit of a heartbeat. There. Did you feel that shift as we bring ourselves into our bodies? Yes, that's it.

"Miriam, bring yourself fully into your heart as if your attention is on the other side of that tapping. It's like you're watching the fingers tap from the inside. That's it. As you bring your attention fully inside, and you feel yourself breathing from inside your heart – inside that cavernous space in your chest – it brings us into this moment. We acknowledge that we're moving more and more and more into this moment. Good. Feel yourself being pulled and drawn to the sacred chamber. Move your attention to that beautiful, sacred place within – that place that's found directly behind the heart and just below it. That's the sacred place of your creation that's in partnership with the Divine. The place of deepest connection to Divine love. Are you there in your sacred chamber, Miriam?"

Miriam diligently following along answers, "I am, thank you."

"Good," I continue, "Do you see that beautiful atmosphere of change as you move into a much deeper form of love, support, light, stillness, peace, and calm? Do you feel that?"

"Yes," answers Miriam.

"Beautiful," I affirm and continue, "Now, we're just kind of soaking in that energy. We soak it in until we become it, until all of this is our universe. Now, as we bring your attention into your body and think about the cancer and the breakdowns and the health issues that you've had for the last seven months, ask into your body, 'Where is that place in my body that would like to talk to me about all this?'"

Qualifying her answer Miriam says, "This sounds bizarre to say, but it's inside my ear."

"Ah, good," I continue. "What does it look like inside your ear?"

"It looks brown, but it's the brown of a lush forest," describes Miriam, "with a lot of brown moss."

"Brown moss," I restate. "What is the emotional sensation there, the feelings sense?"

Miriam is good and present, so we are getting at a lot very quickly in this Spontaneous Transformation.

She says, "When I was in the chamber, it was love, and I wanted to cry. Its wonderment, like there's some light that's supposed to come in, and I just have to find it."

Following along, I check-in and say, "I'm getting an interpretation, and, if this is wrong, please let me know, but it feels like that place of love that wants to make you cry is source energy. It is a profound experience for us to find the light within this three-dimensional space. By light, I mean the love of source energy. Does that feel true to you?"

Miriam confirms my intuition.

"Great," as I circle back, I say, "So, thank you for that beautiful wisdom, that is inside your ear.

"We're in this forest. We're in this place of wonderment and we're looking for the light. Let's just ask the forest, ask the ear, how do we find the light?

Miriam says, "Open our hearts and look up."

"What happens when we open our hearts and look up?" I ask.

"It's all light," Miriam realizes and adds, "already."

I repeat, "It's all light, already."

Miriam adds, "Peace is coming through."

I repeat, "Peace."

Miriam, really in the moment, adds, "There're even animals in the forest, now, and they're all feeling peace."

"Yes," I affirm, "This beautiful energy of peace surrounding you, that is you coming from within, showing itself as this, showing what the world really is.

"Imagine that your body and your health and your expensive mechanical issues and all of these things are in this world. What would happen?"

Miriam quickly knows the right answer for her and states, "I would approach it all with peace."

I ask Miriam to picture something that recently happened, and give an example of it, as I prep her to re-pattern through the Spontaneous Transformation.

"I had some very expensive repairs on my car," says Miriam.

"There you go," tracking Miriam. I continue by saying, "The car breaks down and you're in that moment with not knowing exactly how much it's going to be. What happens now when you come from the forest analogy?" Miriam knows the right answer for herself from this peaceful place, "I feel like whatever it is, the money will be there."

Re-patterning from a place of peace, I say, "Right, okay. Now you find out how much it's going to cost."

Miriam inquiries, "From this place or from the place I was when it actually happened?"

"Exactly," I point out, "There's the glitch. It's a beautiful, beautiful glitch. Here's what you just said, 'from this place, it would be this, but where I am, or where I was, it would be something else.'

"Meaning, you sensed the difference between the forest analogy perception versus your old perception, as if they are different. Do you see the dichotomy between those two? This disconnect is actually perfect because until you know what it is, you can't fix it. I mean, fixing is not the right word. But you can't shift it until you recognize it.

"Now we see the glitch. There's your life over there that you have to deal with, and there's the life in the forest that is another reality, right?"

Following along, Miriam says, "Right."

"Is there anything that I missed?" I ask.

"What's coming up for me is remembering that I felt betrayed because this car shouldn't have that kind of expensive repairs," she explains.

"Ah, beautiful." I say not in regards to the expense of the car, but on her recognition of what the thought was that shifted her out of the peaceful vibration.

"I felt betrayed by my health issues because I believe they shouldn't have happened," she says, adding, "I didn't take full responsibility."

"When you are in the forest, are you in your life?" I ask.

"I can be," Miriam answers.

"What would it look like if you brought the forest energy into your life?" I ask.

"Life would be wonderful," Miriam responds.

"Yes," I affirm. "Let's look at the betrayal aspect. I want you to feel the betrayal of your body because that's what it feels like. It feels like your body betrayed you. Is that true?"

"Yes, it did," Miriam responds.

"So, your body betrayed you, and then your car betrayed you," I point out. "These are things that are just so out of your control, right? So, when we label these things as 'betrayal,' and that's an honest labeling, it's absolutely beautiful and perfect. There's zero judgment here because that was what you were feeling. It was totally the truth for you in that moment: 'This freaking car betrayed me; my body betrayed me.'

"Your body is actually a perfect manifestation of your thoughts and beliefs. It isn't capable of betraying you. Does that feel true?"

"When I'm in the forest, yes," admits Miriam.

"Okay, perfect," refocusing the conversation. "All right, let's look at betrayal. When was the very first time in your life that you felt betrayed? How old were you?"

Remembering, Miriam answers, "Three."

"Bring yourself to that beautiful three-year-old," as I guide Miriam. "Bring yourself as this beautiful, magnificent woman that you are, as the forest woman. Now, there you are with this three-year old, what happened to this three-year-old? The attention that was coming to her was all of a sudden completely dragged away. Is that true?"

"Yes," says Miriam.

"See how powerful you are?" I ask. "We create from this space of perception. So, that happened quite a bit. You just got to experience it again, but this time your three-year-old got to experience it with you hanging out with her. How did that feel?"

"It felt safe," Miriam replied. "No longer any judgment, no longer any question of what was wrong with me that I was 'betrayed.'"

I ask, "What does that feel like for that three-year-old to experience no judgment?"

"Joyous relief," answers Miriam.

"Yes, joyous relief," I affirm. "She feels that joyous relief, knowing that you know what she discovered at three years old – that no one is ever to be blamed and that everyone is doing the best they can. Is that true?"
"Yes," Miriam says, "that is what she feels now."

"Now, just imagine that three-year-old growing up with that understanding," I say.

Then I lead Miriam through the age progression process as part of the re-patterning from this higher vibrational emotional state. The importance is for her mind, body, and emotions to align to this new vibration.

Trauma happens at some point in our youth and gets repeated. This creates a belief loop, and a thought loop which causes the body to repress emotions until the body gets your attention to stop the pattern of looping by showing up as an illness.

Miriam acknowledges that is what it's been feeling like for her since it happened which is why it is helpful to process these big life chunks out with others, when you choose to work Spontaneous Transformation.

Miriam's physical issues and mechanical issues were one hundred percent vibrational resonance with this belief system that she was holding. Now that she has the truth behind both the health issue and the financial trigger, she can continue to work on catching the looping and moving into a higher vibrational space.

Much of the inconveniences and troubles we have in our life are there for us to address the underlying belief systems. In Miriam's case, this was a lifelong pattern. None of the stuff showed up overnight. Miriam was living in two different places. She was living in the place of struggle, and at the same time, the world in the forest. Things were either really good or they were bad.

With Miriam's attempt to re-pattern and commitment to practice Spontaneous Transformation, she gets to bridge the gap between these two conflicting worlds or two conflicting belief systems she was holding onto. She can now have compassion for herself, for her body.

The stunning irony is that it was Miriam's ear that was the clue into letting her know that she was not listening to her body. It really does make you pause and recognize the power of the body when it speaks.

It is such a privilege and just an amazing, awesome experience to witness people's growth. We really do have everything we need within to take care of ourselves and create life just as we want it, so that the surprises are eye-opening in a positive way. I am just a guide in the process for those who feel pulled to take care of themselves in this way.

The same practices and basic principles even apply when it comes to sexual abuse and its mental/emotional/physical manifestations. The body is such a fascinating place of holding and protecting. As we form a healthy, communicative relationship with ourselves, the body no longer has to carry within it that which does not ultimately serve our good.

MOVING BEYOND SEXUAL ABUSE

Sexual abuse is always a very difficult trauma to deal with. It can set up misalignments in the body and spirit that last a lifetime. It can temporarily set up barriers to joy and healthy, loving relationships. It can even make us feel as if we have lost touch with our very being – our soul. Yet, the resulting confusion can also cause us to reach out for a greater understanding of who we really are, ultimately achieving a realization of freedom that virtually dissolves all its associated issues. I have had much personal experience with this, so I bring to you my understanding of how painful it is, my deepest compassion for those who have experienced it, and my knowledge of the journey to realign the physical with the Divine within you.

As with everything else, recognizing what happened to us, and how we store that in our body, is an important part of moving passed it. In order to shift, we must be willing to move beyond our story, and beyond the traumatic imprint we let it establish in our vibrational blueprint. Health begins as we move toward who we really are – beings of light and love. We do this by accessing those traumas first, not re-experiencing them. Then we can realign and re-pattern them into a healthy story that serves our good into the future.

How We Can Stop Re-traumatizing Ourselves

In the late eighties and early nineties, when I was undergoing training as a body worker and healer, the popular therapeutic processes for dealing with sexual abuse were things such as Primal Scream therapy and EST. While observing these processes, I repeatedly witnessed participants re-traumatizing themselves by re-living the experience over and over again. It seemed so brutal and unnecessary to me; it motivated me to leave this training and apply my own system to resolve this issue for myself.

Often, it takes courage to reveal what we have gone through in our past. It is perhaps even more challenging to bring incidents of sexual abuse to light because they take place in a dark place, in an ignored space, where everyone pretended it was not happening. A good way to begin to address the past is by speaking with ourselves first about what happened. We can dialogue with our bodies and, as we feel safe, with our therapists and our trusted friends, whom we know can hold nonjudgmental space for us to share something so personal.

Addressing our abuse – acknowledging that it did happen – is such a large part of ultimately finding peace and harmony in our lives, our bodies and our relationships. For many of us, the memories of our abuse were suppressed or held onto until we were ready to deal with them. Thus, the journey of facing our abuse head-on begins with saying, "Yes that actually did occur." By affirming that you know something took place, even if you are not sure what yet, you automatically align with what your body already knows. It knows that you are listening now. You have forged a bond with yourself that likely felt broken. You have taken the first big step to understanding its place in your life so that you can move beyond it.

When I say "speak it," I don't mean in the sense that you affirm that you were a "victim." I have noticed how some people, with good intention, will share what happened to them in such detail and emotion as if they are reliving it. Rather than using the affirmation as a step toward wholeness, it feels as if they are holding onto the story like, "Yes, that's who I am. There it is. I am a victim." I can tell you from personal experience, you are not "that." Something happened *to* you that allowed you to move into the world in a way that was different and unique. While that was something that happened, it was definitely not the traumatic event that defined you.

The journey of moving beyond sexual abuse through inner dialoguing leads us finally beyond the past traumatic occurrence and into a future of our own making. This does not mean that we deny what happened to us nor suppress what we remember. It means that, once we have addressed the abuse which we've endured, we don't continue to relive the explicit details of what happened. It becomes something that simply happened to us. It is never a reflection of who we are. The pain and confusion is prolonged by believing mistruths about ourselves – that we are powerless, and that what happened to us defines who we are.

The Spontaneous Transformation path returns us to wholeness by reminding us of who we truly are. We have always been our essential, authentic, powerful creator selves – and always will be.

I actually wore my trauma and abuse as a badge of honor and would tell anyone and their brother. What happens when you repeatedly tell the old stories is you just shock a bunch of people and they feel very sorry for you. I would posit that you don't need people feeling sorry for you, because then they are not seeing you as a real, authentic and healthy individual. The opportunity now is to push yourself into the next iteration of you.

Creating a Brand New Story to Realign the Self

Through re-patterning and moving through the truth of who we are, forgiveness can happen. This is not to deny any past or present experience, but to create a brand new story for yourself that yields healthier experiences moving forward.

I couldn't will or force myself to forgive anyone. To be honest, I had no intention of ever forgiving those who hurt me. I have, however, completely forgiven them, but it was unintentional. It happened naturally as I consistently asked for a joyful life, a truer understanding of myself, and to be a vessel for love in the world. In order to be a vessel for love in the world, I had to feel forgiveness. It never required asking anyone to say they were sorry.

Instead, my constant meditation was, "How can I be a vessel for love in the world?" As I focused on this singular question, the faces of those who hurt me showed up along with the emotions that were held in my body from those traumatic experiences. I chose to re-pattern these experiences by feeling the Divine within me, the places of love and light that had been there all along. Then, I moved into a place of allowing a new story to show up. Now, we can't force the little children that we were to cognitively understand a new way of existing in the world. We have to actually experience it. That's what vibrational resonance is. It's having an experience that sets up a new energetic signature in the body that then creates new "good" experiences. By doing my own inner-play, over time, I was able to feel forgiveness. I believe you can, too.

Moving Beyond Sexual Abuse: A Spontaneous Transformation

In the following therapeutic session, Ingrid, a participant in my *MasterWorks Healing Membership Site,* grapples with her own experience with sexual abuse and moves toward a place of realigning her emotions, her beliefs and her sense of identity around a life story that better represents her true essence.

An exhausted Ingrid describes her situation to me, "It's quite complex. My issue is about relationships and my disease, or my chronic exhaustion. I have had this chronic exhaustion for a very long time actually, but it kind of pulls me out of the very destructive relations I keep having with men."

"You have destructive relationships with men, and you have chronic fatigue," I repeat.

"Yes," affirms Ingrid. "The chronic fatigue has taken me away from getting involved with men. It was a good time to recover and relax. It was an excellent time of peace, being alone, living totally free, and having time to do healing work. Now, I am slowly recovering and getting more energy again. I can leave the house sometimes once, or twice a week. I don't have to lie down and rest so much anymore.

"But I'm thinking about the issue with men again. I realize that I have a lot of pain and fear around the thought of getting involved with a man again. I'm not sure which is more important, to heal my issues with men, or healing my chronic fatigue?"

"Ingrid, do you meditate?" I inquire. "What other alternative means are you using to manage your illness?"

"I do so much," she says with another sigh of exhaustion. "I do EFT. I do a lot of Spontaneous Transformation. I do supplements. I do lots of cleansing and colon cleansing."

"How is your gratitude practice?" I ask.

"I'm grateful for my apartment. I live with my mom. My mom took me in because I needed someone to take care of me. I have a wonderful, wonderful relationship with her. I'm very grateful for my wonderful computer because it's my connection to the world. There are so many things that I'm very grateful for. I'm very happy, actually. I started to become happy with this kind of life," she shares.

"Tell me what else you are grateful for," I follow up.

Ingrid gives thanks to the summer birds feeding in her window, but then says, "I'm grateful for the few connections I still have, but not very many..."

I interrupt, "Okay. That's not gratitude. We want a hundred percent gratitude only. Just talk about the connections and don't talk about the fact that there aren't enough. What I'm pointing out here is the use of language, which is simply a barometer for where we're at. I can sense that you do feel gratitude, but the gratitude feels to me like it's coming from your head and not your heart. You will notice this when you listen to this recording again.

"You will notice those times where, 'I'm grateful for the few friends that I have, *but* I don't have very many anymore.' That's not gratitude. That's an indicator of where your energy is at, which is okay. There is nothing wrong with that. It's just an indicator.

"It feels like you are on the verge of moving past chronic fatigue, past destructive relationships, and moving into the world again. Is that something that you want?"

"Yes. I'm very scared. I'm really scared," she shares with me.

I affirm Ingrid by saying, "I get it. That's really important to know that it's not really what you want because it's too scary. Is that true?"

"Yes," she says.

"That's okay," I acknowledge. "Do you see where the intention and the beliefs, 'it's too scary to overcome?' is effecting the creation of your reality?

"You are not going to overcome it from that space. It's impossible. You can't. You can't feel gratitude when you're in that space, as well, because gratitude will put you into flow, which will put you into a life that is too scary. What I want you to understand is that all this stuff you're doing is not going to move you passed this wall.

"I don't mean to be hard on you. I'm just pointing out what is really happening for you right now. It doesn't mean that this can't change in the next five minutes. I also want to point out that it's important to know that the subtleties of our unconscious traumas and beliefs will stop our energy until we're ready. The fact that we're conversing right now means that we're ready. Ingrid, the fact that you are here working with me means that you are ready.

"I want you to feel 'you are ready' in your body. I want you to feel 'you are ready' in your body because you are here right now. Good. There's a little subtle shift there. I want you to feel the strength within that readiness. You're ready. That's a big step. Just knowing that you're ready is a step. Is that true for you?"

"Yes," answered Ingrid.

"Very good. That was a real yes," I affirm. "Right. We're dancing around a trauma. This trauma has created an interesting adventure for you. Okay? What is the date today?"

"Today's date?" Ingrid unsure of where this is going, finally says, "The twelfth of December."

"What time is it right now?" I ask.

"It's ten minutes past eleven in the morning in California," she answers.

"So it's ten minutes past eleven on December 12th. Okay." I confirm, anchoring her into time and space and the now moment.

I continue, "You're here, right now, living in a safe apartment with your mom with beautiful birds that come visit you and your wonderful computer. You're here with us in this moment. Right here, right now you're with us and you're safe. Do you get it? You're right here, right now and you're safe."

"Yes, I am safe," she repeats.

"I want you to look around the room at ten past eleven on December 12th, and see that you are here. Look around at the objects in the room and see that you are here and present right now," I say making sure again that she is locking into this time and space.

"There is the shift. Lovely. Okay. We're going to go into your body from this place of safety, knowing that you're safe on this December 12th. You are here as this beautiful woman all grown up. We're going to move into your body and explore this destructive relationship, this fear of men. Okay?"

"Yes," she says following my guidance.

"Let's create another place of safety. Bring your attention into your heart. I want you to put your hand on your heart and just tap. Thump-thump... thump-thump... thump-thump. Tap a heartbeat. That's it. Bring your attention to your heart. Thump-thump... thump-thump... And then pay attention to your breath. Good. I want you to imagine that you have a nose in your heart. That nose is breathing through your heart. Thump-thump... Tapping your heart. Tapping your chest. That's it. Good. Bring your attention fully into your heart. There we go," as I walk her through the words into her Sacred Chamber.

"Now, I want you to bring your attention to the place just behind your heart. You can stop tapping when it's comfortable. Bring your attention just behind and below your heart. There is a beautiful sacred chamber that's sitting right there. I want you to bring your attention into that beautiful sacred chamber. Do you get a sense of that, Ingrid?"

"Yes," Ingrid says as she follows along.

"As you move into that beautiful place, I want you to feel the support and the safety that is here for you. Feel the support and the safety here. This is your place of deepest connection to source energy. Just feel that support. Feel that connection. This sacred chamber is just one big ball of love. That's what's here for you. That's who you are. Yes, that's it. I want you to really feel the safety here. Do you feel it?"

"Yes," Ingrid says with her hand on her heart. Then she says, "I'm doubting it a bit."

"Doubt doesn't exist in the sacred chamber, so it's more than likely that you are not there," I say making the subtle distinction, "so bring your attention back into the sacred chamber. Now, when you're in that beautiful sacred place, I want you to also remember that you're all grown up, December the twelfth. Combine those two thoughts together. You feel the safety of your apartment, right?"

"Right." She says.

"Right," I repeat. "Feel that safety and then combine it with the connection and source energy that's here in the sacred chamber. There we go. Feel that beautiful sacred energy. There we go. There is that source energy. It is even safer, isn't it?"

"Yes," she assures.

"Because it's your source, which is the ultimate protection that's always there for us, always. There we go. Very nice. Feel the safety and the support that's there for you, knowing that you're all grown up here and now, and you're present and safe right in this moment... There we go. Lovely, Ingrid. Can you feel that?" I ask.

"Yes," as she eases into the process.

"You're really doing well. I'm going to recommend that you listen to this recording every day, and bring yourself to this place of safety," I remind her. "So from this place of safety, knowing today's date, knowing that you're in your sacred chamber and you are surrounded with the love of the Divine, we're going to bring the attention into your body. We are going to bring this safety with us. In every moment, we're going to know that we are surrounded by Divine love of source energy, and that we are in the present moment. As we bring our attention into the body, we're going to ask the body. Where in your body do you feel this tension, this challenge, and this fear of men? Where is that in your body? Where is that in your body?"

"Right now, it's in my upper chest," she says, and I can hear the constriction in her voice.

"What else?" I inquire.

"It's floating into my throat," she says with that continuing tension in her voice.

"Let's bring your attention into your upper chest and throat. Tell me, what does it look like in there?" I ask.

"Like a rubber tube," she answers.

"What is the feeling sense of this rubber tube?" I ask.

"I don't know how to say it. It's not totally tight, but it's very firm," she states.

"So we've got this beautiful – and I'm going to say beautiful because I think it's beautiful that it's showing itself to you – firm rubber tube. Now, let's ask this firm rubber tube why it's here. So, I'm going to ask a couple of questions. Pick the one that feels the best.

"Ask it, 'Why are you here? Or, how have you served me? Or, what is this about?'"

"I don't know," Ingrid says, "I get pain in my chest."

"Yes. So you got some pain there," I restate, "that's good."

"Is pain good?" she says with a tinge of panic in her voice.

"What's today's date Ingrid?" I ask, reminding her of where she is right now.

"It's December 12th," she answers.

"So you've got some pain there," focusing in, I state. "And you're safe and fine in this moment, right?"

"Yes," Ingrid replies.

"I want you to hold the tension between the pain that's in your chest and the fact that you're safe. Just hold the awareness of those two spaces. Can you do that?" I ask.

"Yes," she replies.

"Good, very good, Ingrid. Now I want you to just feel how powerful you are in this moment. Holding the tension of those two things makes you incredibly powerful. Do you feel that sense?" I ask

"Yes," Ingrid says.

My purpose of defining that she is safe and in the moment is that my sense is her body is holding a painful memory that is going to be scary for Ingrid to face. She has to be in charge and in control of the reveal, and not me. She has agreed that she was ready for the memory to surface when I confirmed with her earlier that by being here, she was in fact ready.

"When you listen back to this recording at this point, you will hear how strong your voice sounds, too," reassuringly, I continue guiding her with my voice saying, "So you've got this pain now in your chest when you asked the question, 'What is this about?'"

"What comes up is it's holding me together," she answers, then she repeats, "This rubber tube is holding me together."

"Yes, that's right," I say. "So it has really served you, hasn't it? It has actually helped you. Even though it's painful, it has helped you. Here's what happens. These things are there to protect us. Something got held in there, and the rubber tube came along to hold you together. So we're just going to thank that chest area and that wonderful rubber tube for being so brave and holding you together for so long. How does that feel?"

"It feels strange that I can thank it," she says, "but it still hurts."

"That's okay. We're not asking it to change. We're just showing gratitude for it. 'Thank you so much for protecting me. Thank you. Thank you. Thank you. Thank you. Thank you. Thank you, rubber tube, for protecting me.' There we go. 'Thank you. Thank you. Thank you. Thank you. Thank you,'" I say repetitively.

"I can feel how difficult the shift is because I am fighting it, and not wanting to thank it," she admits.

"That's understandable. Just have gratitude for that beautiful tube. It did protect you. I want you to feel how much it protected you. It really did protect you. It held on to something until you were ready, which we discovered this morning that you're ready, that you are powerful, that you are holding the tension here between this moment in time and this area that's ready to be released. So, we're going to thank that beautiful rubber tubing for protecting you, and holding it together. It held you together, didn't it?"

"Yes," she says with focus.

With fierce intent I say to her and to the rubber tube, "Thank you for holding Ingrid together. Thank you. Can you say that Ingrid?"

"Thank you for holding me together," she repeats with ferocity.

"There we go. Did you feel that? That was a nice little release there. Has it changed at all?" I ask.

"The pain is gone," she says with surprise.

"So there's a little bit of freedom in there now," I say. "That is good."

"It feels tighter in the throat now," she says with worry.

"So let's follow that energy, 'It's tighter in the throat'," staying real close to the energy as she speaks. "So, let's just go to the throat area and ask that area. How has it served you, in your throat? Or, what is this about?"

"Suffocation comes up," she says.

"Suffocating," I repeat. "So, what's the date today?"

"December twelfth," she says.

"We have the safety of the sacred chamber there powerfully supporting you. That's very good, Ingrid," I say reassuringly. "That's very good. I want you to feel how powerful you are right in this moment. It's all okay. So there's suffocating happening here in the throat. The suffocating is real. It happened. I want you to know that you're present here right in this moment. Is that true?"

Trusting the process, Ingrid says, "Yes."

"It feels like this is both a past life thing and a current life thing. Tell me if this feels true. If it doesn't feel true, then I am happy to go with what you're feeling. But, it kind of feels like it's a past life. It feels like something also happened in this lifetime that you may not remember. Do those two things feel true to you?" I ask.

"Yes. I have been orally abused, and I suffocated" she states.

"Okay. So you were suffocated in this lifetime," I restate.

"Yes," she says, "about the past life, I don't know."

"It feels like there was something that happened in the past life with the same person who abused you in this lifetime," I say with contemplation. "So, let's talk to the throat or the rubber tubing, 'We understand that there's some suffocation and there's abuse here. We understand that the rubber tubing likely held you together from the abuse. We thank the beautiful throat for sharing with us right now the suffocation. It's sharing with us what it experienced, what the tissues experienced, and what you experienced.'

"We're just going to have some gratitude now for the rubber tubing holding it for you until this moment, until a moment when you're completely safe and supported. You're supported not only in your home by your mother, but also by this community. Okay?"

"Yes," Ingrid says with some emotion.

I say, "I want you to feel right now how strong you are. Do you feel that?"

"Yes," she says.

"You're this powerful, beautiful woman who's ready to explore and realign this to a new experience. Does that feel true?" I ask.

"Yes," she says.

"Good, very good, Ingrid. That was a nice claim," I acknowledge and continue guiding, "Let's ask the throat and the heart. 'What do you need?' Ingrid, what does your throat and the rubber tubing need now?"

"Release," she says.

"Okay, good," I say knowing she's making progress. "Release. It needs release. Let's ask it very clearly, very succinctly, the following question: What would release look and feel like? What would release look and feel like?"

"Opening up and becoming soft," she says.

"So, what would that look and feel like?" I ask.

"Relaxing, releasing, and breathing," she says as she starts to relax, release, and breathe.

"So what would breathing and relaxing, opening and releasing, look and feel like now?" I ask. "I want you to feel those things – opening, breathing, relaxing, releasing. What do they look and feel like right now in your body, right in this moment? Feel that, Ingrid. Feel that opening, breathing, relaxing, in that area. What does that look and feel like?"

"There are no words. It's just the space I'm only in when I meditate," she says.

"So claim that space now and breathe into it. Feel your chest breathe into that space. Feel your throat breathe into that space," after a pause for breath I continue, "Good. Feel that expansion that's now in your throat and chest, expanding down your arm, down your torso, and throughout your whole body. Your whole body now becomes this place of opening, breathing, relaxing, releasing. Good. Now that we're in this place of openness and breathing and relaxing and releasing, we're going to connect back into the throat and the chest. Tell me, what does it look like in there, now?"

"It's still there, but it's a bit lighter and softer," she confides.

"Well, the rubber hose is keeping you together. So it's an important piece of you in this moment. Let's ask the hose if there's anything else that it needs," I say. "Let's ask it. 'Is there anything else that you need, right now?'"

"Something strange came up," she says with caution, "I don't know where this comes from inside of me, but it's saying to stay away from men."

I repeat, "Stay away from men," and continue, "Good. Now, I want you to know that this feeling that you're having right now, and what you're hearing, is a core pattern for you. You're managing it right in this moment with tremendous power and strength. I want you to feel that. Feel how powerful you are while you're experiencing this core issue. It's really incredible, Ingrid, how strong and powerful you are as you're holding the tension of this moment. Do you get a sense of that?"

"Yes," she says.

"So I'm just going to share something with you... there's tremendous freedom within that power. The more that you play with this energy of safety and opening and releasing and breathing and relaxing, the more you will have power over the idea of staying away from men, and it will no longer have power over you. 'Stay away from men' will become a non-issue.

"Let's just play a little bit with this notion of 'stay away from men.' Let's just ask the rubber hose what it needs around that. What does it need around this notion of staying away from men? What is that statement really about? What does it really need?"

Ingrid answers, "Security and safety."

"Yes, security and safety," I repeat. "That's what that statement 'stay away from men' actually means. It means you want safety and security. Let's just do a quick little visualization here. We're going to go into fantasyland. In this fairyland, Ingrid experiences safety, security and support from men. Complete fantasy, one hundred percent pretend here. It's like we're writing a little novel, a little fictional novel. Okay?"

"Yes," she says curiously.

"Good. What does that land look like?" I ask. "You've walked into the land. There you are, standing fully, beautifully, firmly, completely safe, completely secure with wonderful men that are showing up to support you in that energy. Describe what you're experiencing there in this beautiful fantasyland. What does it feel like to be completely supported and safe with a man? I want you to feel the energy of the opening and the breathing and relaxing and the releasing what you are experiencing here in fantasyland. Nothing can happen to you here.

"You are in this fantasyland where men are lovely, supportive protectors, and providers. Their only job is to protect and provide for Ingrid. What does that feel like, Ingrid? I want you to feel it fully in your body that we have officially claimed that this land is where men protect and provide and deliver security and safety. What does that feel like? What does your body feel like in this land?"

"I can't get there really," she says struggling to follow along.

"Okay. Do you want to play fantasyland?" I ask.

"Yes. I try to imagine it, and the moment I imagine men around me, it actually comes back," she explains.

"Let's create a land that is a hundred percent fantasy. I want you to walk into the land. When you walk into this land, you're going to leave behind any other belief. So, leave this belief at the door as you kick off your shoes. All beliefs and old traumas are just simply left at the door." I say talking with a voice of positive anticipation.

"Now, joy is coming up," says Ingrid.

"There you go," I say. "It is joy and laughter. I want you to feel in your body this joy and this laughter. Feel it moving through you as you are in the land where men are safe. Feel it moving through you in the land where men are protectors and providers. Good."

"Now, there comes a wave of sadness," as she starts to cry.

"You are doing great Ingrid," I reassure her. "Feel that sadness, it's very important to feel, and allow it to pass, and release. That's all. It's not bad. It's just sadness. It's just a feeling. So, feel that feeling of sadness."

"I feel a sadness that I never experienced before," she says as a deep cry ensues.

"Well, that's not sadness, that's grief," I say, "That's very real because this world of abuse does actually exist. The more that you visit this world and create the energy within your world to face this experience; the more this new world will actually show up. I know, I've had personal experience with this, Ingrid.

"I had a very similar experience in my life where there was no way that I could ever be with, or trust, a man. I didn't even like them. I have since come to an understanding and a place of release. I have created amazing men in my life, amazing men. I had no idea these men were out there. Men that really are protectors and providers. Men who really are safe and deliver security. It's real. This land is real. This land is actually within you. When you embrace this land, you create it. That is the law of attraction. That is vibrational resonance.

"So, your assignment, Ingrid, is to visit this land and just allow yourself to slowly but surely increase this vibrational resonance. Allow yourself slowly, but surely, to increase this sense within you of what it feels like to be safe with men. As you listen to this over and over again, you can incorporate this exercise as part of your daily practice. Eventually, you will get to a place where there's more evidence of this land. People will show up like a delivery boy, or a taxi driver. They are all over the place.

"In fact, men are built to be protectors and providers. That's all they want to be. The healthier versions of men just want to make women happy. There are definitely unhealthy versions out there. A really good resource for you is Allison Armstrong's work, PAX, she runs a series called, Understanding Men, and I really love her work.

"Start listening to supportive information about reframing your position around men. They use a very profound analogy in one of the PAX workshops, Men & Sex, where they described some men as sheepdogs; these men are the provider-protectors. Sheepdogs. They are the men that are solid, beautiful and just want to make a woman happy. It just brings tears to my eyes because I finally know this to be true. I know it now in my own heart.

"There are men who are also wolves. These are men that have been damaged. These are men that are not in their provider-protector selves. They've been hurt, damaged, and wounded. They are walking around expressing those wounds. Now, the bottom line is even those men are not misbehaving. They have a really good reason for doing what they're doing, even though it doesn't feel good. It's also important to realize that the wolf and the sheepdog have the same teeth, if that's all you're looking at. The sheepdog might growl because it is going to protect you from those who might hurt you. The wolf will growl because it's dangerous. If all you're looking at is their teeth, that's all you're going to see. If you move your perspective back, you will be able to see the sheepdog as this beautiful protector-provider. That was a really important thing for me to hear because I was relating to all men as the wolf. I realized that there are great, wonderful men in the world. There are wonderful sheepdogs in the world."

In this Spontaneous Transformation session, the "fantasyland" Ingrid stepped into represents the place where she now creates a new story around men and relationships and what could take place there. She entered a realm where endless possibilities exist and she decides what she wants, while still feeling safe. This is also where she can learn how to take care of herself in "the real world." Her body can know how it would feel to be in a safe relationship, which gives her brand new reference points for the future. While life, itself, may not always feel like this fantasyland, the vibrational resonance she creates there allows her to accept more positive experiences from a foundation of self-love, support and healthy choices.

Realigning with the Divine

If it's challenging, even for your imagination, to go to this place of perfect harmony and beauty with close or intimate relationships, it may be that you have disowned certain aspects of yourself along the way. Trauma can do that. To leave behind the pain, we tend to leave behind parts of ourselves. We end up doing exactly what we don't want others to do to us – we abandon ourselves. In an act of attempted self-protection, we believe we will be safer if we don't show up one hundred percent, thinking there may be less of us there to be hurt. Actually, the more whole and present we are, the safer we are.

In the past, it felt as if every moment of trauma in my life made another little piece of me break off. Every moment of trauma created a bit of separation from me and from others, too. I stopped sharing my story with others because it stopped feeling like my story anymore. When I made my life about becoming a vessel for love in the world, my heart had to make room by getting rid of what was still there, taking up space. I was now asking how I could experience more joy, so the story didn't serve my purpose anymore.

As the story lost its power, and love occupied a larger and larger space in my life, I did have a huge moment of forgiveness for the people who "did this to me." What happened in that moment was surprising – the clouds didn't part, the angels didn't sing, and I wasn't all of a sudden miraculously a new person. I felt the experience of forgiveness, which is release. It was also total freedom. I didn't force it. I forgave when it was time, when I felt a beautiful heart opening. I saw those from my past as partners I came here to learn with. Then, I felt different in my life. I had more compassion for everyone in my life. That was a beautiful thing, but everything that happened to me had still happened to me. It took me several years to see that "what happened to me" is also what allowed me to get to this place. If it hadn't happened, I wouldn't have had the extreme focus and dedication to shift my energies and change my life. I would not have had such a deep experience of what it is to forgive.

Completeness is about bringing awareness back to body parts from which we cut ourselves off energetically. For me, it felt like retrieving aspects of the soul.

Many of us have experienced trauma in one form or another, and quite extreme. My feeling is that most of us, who move through it to another place, who deliberately learn to direct energy, become so powerful. We have had so much pain and resistance to work through, we become stronger and more aware than we might have been if we had not experienced the trauma. Many of us are now acting as the catalysts and the guides to wholeness and holiness because of our intimate understanding of how to realign energies and stay in our hearts. And, now, many of us are connecting with each other to combine our energies, and to help others so we can bring wholeness and holiness to the planet as well.

Our heart is really what overcomes any trauma. We release trauma by simply experiencing our heart. The Spontaneous Transformation demonstrates a path for our consistent release of trauma by pursuing our desires from that place of the heart; and to create intention and openness and awareness that allow our brains and our minds to serve as wonderful partners on our path. Here, we generate our own moments of clearing from past trauma. Continue to do this work as long as you need. What I'd like to do now is teach you a powerful process for you to experience completeness and soul retrieval.

What does that mean, soul retrieval? It means this:

We can now take back those aspects of our true essence that were lost to us, that we repressed or hid away from everyone, even ourselves. It means we get to feel whole again, to recall the wholeness which we are, and remember our holiness.

The Wholeness That Creates Holiness: Practice

This process for soul retrieval came, in part, from shamanic work I did for several years. You cannot do this practice enough times. Each time, you allow yourself to release deeper and deeper. So, let's just play with the idea of release and completion here.

1) *Go back into your heart, where all transformation and energetic realignment takes place.*

Do the pearl meditation or whatever it takes to move your awareness back into the sacred chamber – that beautiful space just behind the heart where you know you are safe and loved.

As you move into this beautiful place, feel whatever you feel. If there are tears there, that's okay. Tears are simply for releasing. Open into our heart space and feel the tears, the trauma that's been released, this trauma that's been realigned into love; we've moved through something and remembered who we are as beings of love.

2) *Let your intention be known: you are here to know wholeness and completeness.*

We hold an intention now – intentions, remember how strong intentions are? As we move into our heart space, into that sacred chamber within, we feel the beautiful, divine love that's there just waiting for us. It's been waiting for us. There's a depth there that wasn't there just an hour ago. Even if you can't feel that depth, feel the essence, the inkling. Notice the inkling of the depth. As you feel that beautiful heart space, that sense of knowing, that sense of trust and support that's here for you and has always been here for you, we feel that moment of contentedness as the brain settles down, happy. Like a dog, and it's walking around, around, and around in its bed finding that perfect, golden moment of comfort. It lies there, waiting for the heart to ask for help, but sleeping restfully. In that moment, we ask our beautiful body to receive any pieces, any aspects that left us. Let them know that you understand they left for good reason. You are now ready to welcome them back into this safe haven of this beautiful body with its heart opened and its presence and clarity known.

You can put your intention into the form of a question like, *What would it feel like to feel whole and complete?*

3) *Invite those pieces of the self back into wholeness.*

Those aspects left us because they had to. Now we have created this sacred ground for them to move back into us, moving back into us, those many, many aspects that broke away. We welcome them as if we're in this beautiful hall, and we welcome them with open arms. Welcome, beautiful piece of my heart. Welcome, beautiful piece of my body. Welcome, beautiful aspect of my being that left me, because you had to in order to protect me and to keep that aspect whole, and now it's coming back. It's moving in. Thank you, beautiful mind. It's an aspect of my mind, of all of our minds, that is coming back, and there's an aspect of our being moving in. The beautiful pieces are floating in and we welcome them in celebration. There's a big party happening in our hearts as we welcome these pieces back, as we have the power and the strength and the willingness in this moment to be able to contain these pieces. As these pieces come back, they add to our strength and power and resilience and love. They're bringing back the innocent aspects of love that we lost but have now found.

4) *Accept and adjust to wholeness.*

They move back into our body, into our being, into our soul. They move back into us. There's a big party in heaven and on earth. There's a big party in our beautiful, whole soul, welcoming these old friends – welcoming these old friends back into our being as we are made whole – and we are made whole. We feel that completeness within our being. I didn't even notice that piece was gone, and it feels so good now that it's back. I didn't know I'd lost you. Thank you for coming back. I want to thank all the pieces that left us, knowing that they had to, to protect us, to keep that beautiful aspect alive, and now they're back, reminding us again of who we are as innocent beings of light and love; innocent, powerful beings, emissaries of the divine. These aspects remind us again of who we are. It feels like we just say, "Oh, and so it is – and so it is." Take a very deep breath. Make a noise and smile as you breathe out. As you do that, feel your body expand and reconnect to these pieces. Every breath in actually expands, and every breath out expands it even more.

5) *Stay within this expanded experience of yourself to establish it within your body/mind.*

This is your true state. Stay with this new experience of wholeness for as long as you can hold onto it. If anything wants to retreat or shy away, or if you feel they are not safe here, repeat the earlier process of creating a new story in the land of pretend. The imagination is just another entry point, another door to your holiness.

We are all capable of opening up to greater and greater experiences of love and security and healthy, happy relationships. By going inside to this safe, sacred place to tell a different story, you find what is true for you. You become more discerning because you know how to listen to your needs. You develop a self-nurturing communication system within and bond tighter with yourself. You realign the self and bring your wholeness to the past. Now, you are ready to live that into your future.

EPILOGUE

RESONATING ABUNDANCE and JOY DAILY

Having resolved a range of deep issues, you have cleared a great deal of space to now know abundance and joy. These are higher energies which you can resonate with on a daily basis. The practices within this chapter get you intimately familiar with the feeling of joy and abundance within your body so that you recalibrate your energetic "set point." Because we can have a tendency to slip back into old ways of feeling and thinking, this chapter focuses on replacing old patterns of lack with the experience of abundance. You will also do a final clearing of any residual sense of lack that still persists within the body. This establishes and grounds your attraction point from here onward.

Moving Into Flow

Like every other feeling, a sense of lack resides in the body. It can be just as easily replaced as any other unwanted feeling with better feelings and thoughts. Having realigned the Self with the Divine, the resulting wholeness, joyful living and abundance from day to day and moment to moment comes naturally. This is what it is to move into flow.

Mary A. Hall and I developed this particular practice for letting go of a feeling of lack. Our natural ability to visualize using our imagination, which we use every day, is incredibly powerful. This is an easy letting-go exercise that will make room for you to accept you're good. As we do any visualization work, the mind feels everything that we say. That work is important because the body feels, as we move this energy out, that it literally moves the perceived bad energy out.

We start by moving into the sacred chamber, a place in your body that you are hopefully familiar with by now. It's important that you begin a regular practice of hanging out in your sacred chamber. Strengthen that connection you feel there. If an occasion does throw your energy "off," or if you find your resonance "off" over time, always return to this sacred place, and make it a regular practice. It can be a refuge for you to get back to square one then recalibrate back to what you want. The more you go there and get familiar with it, the easier and easier it becomes to access this safe place of peace.

Knowing Abundance and Joy: Practice

Practicing the Pearl Meditation is one of the best tools to know abundance and joy in your heart. For those of you who are feeling that connection, nod your head toward that connection. Get familiar with it. Feel gratitude in your heart that you are capable of making this connection. If you do not yet feel the connection, please trust that the connection is there. Simply practice without expectation. At the end of this meditation, when we move back into the chamber, you will likely feel it. This connection to source energy, and to yourself, is always there. Every one of us is connected. Feel into that space of peace and support and love and safety.

Next, we're going to bring our attention into our body. I want you to notice that you're in your chamber, and you're moving your attention from the chamber into the body. As you do this, you have a sense of safety and peace as you know the connection is there.

Recall a time in your life when you felt particularly in the flow. You felt peace and joy and love, or any one of those things. This is what abundance feels like. For every one of us, even if we've had challenging lives, there's at least one moment that we can reflect back on when everything worked. Everything we wanted fell right into place, easily and effortlessly. We were in the flow. It felt natural and good and everything you needed came in to support you.

Now, move into that feeling place of peace and abundance that you may have experienced before. Acknowledge the deep sense of safety and joy that you have felt somewhere before. Feel it again. Now bring your whole body into this. What were you emotionally feeling? What comes to mind? Peace? Love? Joy? What is the sensation that you are having? What does it smell like? Are you outside? Are you inside? What are you feeling when you feel this moment of safety and joy and peace and abundance?

Feel into that. Allow that sensation to fill your whole body. Let it spill into every corner and crevice of your body. Feel joy and abundance flowing through your veins. Allow that to nudge all of the non-responsive cells in your body into this higher vibration so that you can almost detect your body humming with a wonderful warmth and flow. Feel that sense of abundance.

Let's move the energy of that moment into the present, so that you can feel and grow that memory muscle. Become aware of your present. Hold the sensation of the moment and what is happening around you along with your inner experience of joy and abundance. Feel into that. Acknowledge this as a real experience, happening now, in this place at this time. Allow that sense of abundance and joy that you felt once before to grow within you. Recognize this feeling as one you can recreate. Move your mind's attention to every part of your body as if you are memorizing how the body holds joy.

You have carried a lot of things in your life and you have, within these processes, let go of those same things. Now, it's time to choose to carry love and joy with you at all times. Remember how this feels and return to its imprint within your body, within your heart and within your mind as peace and abundance. This is who you are.

Clear and Cleanse Lack: Practice

Sometimes, when we raise our resonance, it's like shining a light into the corners of our heart and mind. Pockets of leftover resistance that we didn't know we still carried can be revealed. This last practice gives you the chance to clear and cleanse any leftover sense of lack you may hold onto. You can include this practice within the process of *Knowing Abundance and Joy,* or do it on its own, whenever disbelief arises. This process is also perfect to utilize after doing a cleansing exercise such as Ho'oponopono because it creates an openness in our body and allows us to move into a deeper level of concentration and expanded flow.

1) *Check into the body and locate any residual sense of lack.*

In case you are not feeling this joy one hundred percent, I want you to feel into your body, into a place that may not believe in the feeling of abundance. Ask yourself if there is a place in your body that's saying, "I'm not so sure about this?" Or a place in your body that is complaining a bit or doesn't want to come along and be a part of your new, emerging joy. It may be a place of tension. It may be a place of pain or it may be dark, like there's a void there. It may also be a place that's quite emotional.

2) *Move your attention to that place; observe and acknowledge what is.*

Where exactly in your body are you feeling this? Move your attention to that area, spot, feeling or voice in your body. There might be a couple of places, but there's one in particular that's calling you right now. You are going to have a little conversation with that place. I want you to move your attention into that place. As you move your attention to that place, ask yourself, in your mind's eye or out loud: What does it look like? Is there a sense or emotion in there? Is there a color? You might even get the sense that an object is in there or a voice. It could be the voice of someone else or you at another time in your life.

You're safe, right here, right now. Please know that the sacred chamber energy is with you. A painful memory may come up, but you don't have to go into the memory. What we're doing is simply noticing. You are observing. You already know who you are. You are just simply bringing your awareness to what is. Remember when I talked about the observer effect earlier in the book? That principle applies here. All we're doing is watching. We're just watching. We're just noticing.

Do you sense a shift that happened there just by your observing? This is the power of the body. When the body feels heard, it has a chance to release.

So, right now, you're in a place of listening and being present with that part of your body that is not convinced. You are present with that part of your body that is actually a little focused on lack, or the part that moves you into a place of lack. So where in your body are you feeling that? What does it look like in that place?

3) *Dialogue with what's present to discover what it needs.*

Now that you know what it looks like and have described it to yourself, go ahead and ask that area two questions: What is this about? (Or what is going on here?)

Also ask, what do you need? Feel into it. What does this area need?

When you get an idea of what it needs, it might be a word. It might be a word like support, acknowledgment, and love. You may get a sensation or image that conveys its need. If it's an object, it may need for the object to be removed. If it is a feeling that you are dealing with, it may be that the feeling sense needs to be removed. Just ask it what it needs and stay attentive to listen. It will always respond, so trust what you get. If you feel you're not getting an answer, keep your attention here and ask again. The shift may take place anyway.

4) *Ask the body what it would look or feel like to experience that need fulfilled.*

Once you have a handle on what it needs, ask it another question: What does that look like? Or, what would that feel like?

In other words, you want it to show you its own transformation. If you felt like it needed love or support, what does support look like for that area? What would it feel like to experience love in that area? Go with the need your body just expressed.

5) *Experience the shift and release. Let any remaining resistance be cleared and cleansed.*

Now, allow that to happen. Just as we brought in that energy of love, that memory of love, bring that energy into this area.

If you have a need to release something, imagine a big, beautiful glass ball sitting over your left shoulder. What color is it? This is actually quite a large glass ball, built to hold some of the things we need to release. On the ball, there is a little trapdoor opening. And there is also a little vacuum attachment placed within that opening. Now, the universe is going to act as the vacuum, and pull out those things that you are ready to release. Let all resistance be cleared and cleansed.

Place anything you are ready to simply let go of into the ball. It might be energy or a memory. Then, you're going to move that energy out. The ball has started a vacuum effect. It knows exactly what needs to be removed. It might be an object or a memory of a person that needs to go into that ball. Anything that is ready to be released moves into that ball.

You are pulling it all out and letting it go. As you move this energy into the ball, you're starting to feel lightness in that area that is releasing. Just move more out into the ball. Some areas in your body might be holding tension as well. Now, those areas are releasing that energy into the ball. Letting it go. Moving it out. Letting it go. Releasing it.

The ball is helping you. You can even envision a vacuum sucking all of this energy out into the ball. I want you to feel these shifts in your body. This is real. The sensations you're feeling in your body right now are real. You are creating them. They are not just happening randomly. You can change them as you change your thoughts. When you acknowledge them, the body just feels, "Thank you so much."

6) *Allow perfect joy and lightness of energy to refill the body.*

When the body is free of tension and resistance, the ball is going to close. This ball has a special connection with the sun. The sun is pulling that ball toward it. The sun is this beautiful miracle. The energy of the sun is energy of joy. That's why things grow and transform within its radiant light. This ball moves into the sun and the rays start to hit it. As the rays illuminate the ball, everything inside of it, all that stuff you released, is transmuted and transformed into pure love and joy.

Not only has that negative energy you were holding been released from your body, but that energy has also shifted as it was absorbed into the sun. There is no residue left. The sun has helped all of it transform. It's all gone. Now you have the choice. You can open up the ball and let the energy just release into the universe. Or, you can let the transmuted energy of love and joy move back into your body and fill those spaces that you released.

You can also choose to let some of that energy out into the universe and into you. For those of you who are letting it fall back into your body, just allow it to fill those places. Know that it's transformed love and joy filling you up, creating that sensation in all of your cells.

As you feel that energy of pure love and joy, you recognize it as your own. It is part of you. It has always been part of you. Now it has the space to fill your heart and radiate from within you. You can feel your own energy has completely shifted.

7) *Return to that area of the body to thank it; ground this new experience.*

I want you to just feel into that area again. Feel how it has shifted and changed. Take a moment of gratitude for your body right now. The body held onto old trauma so that you could be protected, so that you wouldn't have to think about it all of the time. Now you can recognize that your body is not the enemy, but it is there to support you. It holds onto things until you're ready to release them.

Keep your attention in that sacred chamber. I want you to feel as if within the sacred chamber there is an oasis in nature. Feel your bare feet in nature, whether they are standing in sand or grass or whatever. Feel your feet on the earth. Roots sprout out of your tailbone and travel all the way down your legs and into to your feet. These roots shoot out of your feet. Your posture is straight as this happens.

These roots are moving deep, deep within the earth. They are moving down to where the best nutrients in the ground are located. The water and the minerals and the nutrients are all there to create a beautiful, healthy, whole body that's in flow and vibrational resonance with abundance. You are going to receive all of these nutrients from the earth. These nutrients are coming up through your roots, up through your feet. As the nutrients travel up your body, a warm sensation pulses through your veins. It looks like energy is moving up into your body, filling you up, filling all your cells. Your cells are drinking in the sensation and the feeling. Now, it's part of your body. Its transformative energy and you allow it to transform your energy.

As that energy really starts to flow, you can also notice warmth from the sun on your skin, your scalp, your back. That sun now moves in and brings the nutrients of light and vitamin D into your body. The energy of lightness moves through your body, intermingling with the energy of the earth's groundedness. At the same time, you're feeling grounded, and you're feeling a lightness. These energies are dancing with one another in your body, filling your cells. Your cells are drinking in the sunlight and drinking in the earth nutrients. You feel this incredible balancing between those two energies. Feel a new balance and rhythm reside within.

I want you to bring your attention back into the room. Just start noticing the objects around you. Start feeling your butt on the couch or whatever it's on. Shake your hands and feet a little bit. Open your eyes. Thank the universe for the experience you just had.

Moving Forward and Resonating What You Want

Your exercise is to revisit this moment, and this sensation, over and over again in order to stay familiar with abundance in your body on a daily basis so that it takes root and grows. It will come to replace any smallness or any sense of lack that tries to return to the body.

You were drawn to read this book because you are ready to release anything else that is *not* you. Your body and soul were ready for something new and different. You were ready to release everything that no longer served you. I hope your journey through this book has, at the very least, awakened your connection to your body. From my experience, however, in my healing practice and on my own journey of using these practices personally, the potential of the Spontaneous Transformation to utterly transform the body is limitless because it is completely self-directed. Our body is the emotional filter through which we consciously experience life. As we learn to listen to our body, we learn to tap into the intuitive guide within, our authentic, fullest expression of ourselves. As we learn to access our trauma and release it, we access the truth of who we are. As we stay rooted in this truth, we begin to live authentically. As we live authentically, the life we have always wanted will show up. What more could we hope for on this juicy life adventure than to authentically traverse the landscape of ourselves and the life we get to experience?

Many of us on this journey got confused along the way. We thought there was a brass ring outside ourselves to reach for and grasp. We went into "doing" mode to "get there." We began to ask the incessant question, "What do we need to do to get this brass ring?" This became the purpose of our lives, and we persistently looked outside ourselves for what we thought we needed in order to be happy, safe, wealthy, and healthy. Perhaps we felt these elusive feelings from time to time, but always temporarily. Maybe we even reached a few brass rings along the way. Yet, we still found that something inside of us was crying out for more. But what? And where could we find it?

Here is the very simple truth: YOU are the brass ring. YOU are the gift for which you are searching. Now you have a path, an opening, into everything you have ever wanted. You know exactly where to find anything you need at all times. Continue to look within. You will never cease to be amazed at the gifts you find and how your acceptance of them has the power to transform your life.

ABOUT THE AUTHOR

JENNIFER MCLEAN

Jennifer has been a healer for twenty years. She trained in various modalities before creating her own healing method – the Spontaneous Transformation. Her healing process has been featured in the book, *The Key,* by notable author Dr. Joe Vitale. Jennifer also produces and hosts an international online series, *Healing With The Masters,* where she interviews the leaders in New Thought and Human Potential. She is also the facilitator of the membership site MasterWorksHealing.com, where she conducts group-coaching sessions based on Spontaneous Transformation and provides a space for prominent healers to use their unique techniques in one-on-one sessions with members in a group-coaching environment. Jennifer has also written *The Big Book of You,* a spiritually and visually inspiring coffee table book full of poetry, photography and insight. She applies Spontaneous Transformation to entrepreneurs to create a new paradigm of "business-from-the-heart" through her Success Signature program: www.SuccessSignature.com.

If you would like more information on Jennifer's healing techniques and the healing materials available, please visit www.mcleanmasterworks.com. If you enjoyed the Spontaneous Transformation sessions throughout this book, taken from *MasterWorks Healing Membership Site,* or if you would like to work personally with Jennifer in a group-coaching environment, you can join here at a discount: **www.SpontaneousTransformation.com.**

PUBLISHED BY TVGUESTPERT PUBLISHING

(Previously Jacquie Jordan Inc. Publishing)

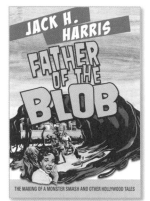

JACK H. HARRIS
Father of the Blob: The Making of a Monster Smash and Other Hollywood Tales
Paperback: $16.95
Kindle/Nook: $9.99

New York Times Bestselling Author, CHRISTY WHITMAN
The Art of Having It All: A Woman's Guide to Unlimited Abundance
Paperback: $16.95
Nook/Kindle: $9.99
Audible Book: $13.00

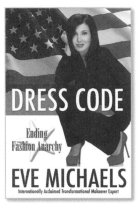

EVE MICHAELS
Dress Code: Ending Fashion Anarchy
Paperback: $15.95
Kindle/Nook: $9.99
Audible Book: $17.95

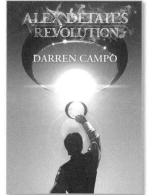

DARREN CAMPO
Alex Detail's Revolution
Paperback: $9.95
Hardcover: $22.95
Kindle: $9.15

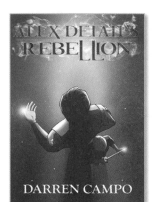

DARREN CAMPO
Alex Detail's Rebellion
Hardcover: $22.95
Kindle: $9.99

DARREN CAMPO
Disappearing Spell
Kindle: $2.99

TVGuestpert Publishing
11664 National Blvd, #345
Los Angeles, CA. 90064
310-584-1504
www.TVGPublishing.com

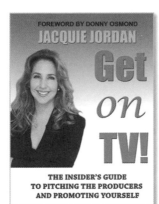

JACQUIE JORDAN
*Get on TV! The Insider's Guide
to Pitching the Producers and
Promoting Yourself*
Published by Sourcebooks
Paperback: $14.95
Kindle: $9.99   Nook: $14.95

JACQUIE JORDAN
*Heartfelt Marketing:
Allowing the Universe to
be Your Business Partner*
Paperback: $15.95
Kindle: $9.99
Audible Book: $9.95

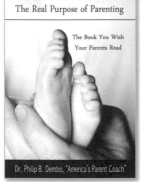

DR. PHILIP DEMBO
*The Real Purpose of Parenting: The
Book You Wish Your Parents Read*
Paperback: $15.95
Kindle/Nook: $9.99
Audible Book: $23.95

CHELSEA KROST
*Nineteen: A Reflection of My
Teenage Experience in an Extraor-
dinary Life: What I Have Learned,
and What I Have to Share*
Paperback: $15.95
Kindle: $9.99
Audible Book: $14.95

DR. JEFF SCHWEITZER
The New Moral Code
Hardcover: $22.95
Audible Book: $17.95